The Ticket

To Terri,
Thanks for having me
on Channel 3 this A.M.
Hope you enjoy the travels
through 'The Ticket'
All the best,
Jack Newcomb
7-1-97

The Ticket

A Fifty-Year Sports Odyssey

BY

JACK NEWCOMB

PREMIUM PRESS AMERICA

Nashville, Tennessee

The Ticket: A Fifty-Year Sports Odyssey
By Jack Newcomb

ISBN 1-887654-25-9
Library of Congress Catalog Card Number 96-71357

PREMIUM PRESS AMERICA books are available at special discounts for premiums, sales promotions, fund-raising, or educational use. For details contact the Publisher at P.O. Box 159015, Nashville, TN 37215-9015; or phone 800/891-7323.

Editor: John Perry & Associates
Assistant editor: Melissa A. Chronister
Layout: Armour&Armour
Cover photo: Hatcher & Fell
Cover design: Armour&Armour
Printed by Vaughan Printing

First Edition, June 1997

1 2 3 4 5 6 7 8 9 10

Contents

Continued on next page

Dedication

My dad got me started on the journey to over eight hundred sporting events fifty years ago. For that I'll always be grateful.

Four generations of ladies have been a source of encouragement and inspiration over the years:

My mother coined the term that has followed me the last several years, "Son, you have a Ticket Fairy," and another comment on my addiction to sporting events, "Boy, you think they can't play without you being there!" Thanks for understanding.

My wife, Ginger, has offered only her encouragement in my pursuits, whether she was included, or interested, or would rather have been baby-sitting grandchildren. She's the best partner a man could have.

My daughter Morna has generously fed my addiction with airline passes and tickets on several occasions. She always makes her old poppa proud.

My five-year-old granddaughter Zara now offers a balance to my fifty years of insanity in chasing The Ticket. I introduced Zara to the Olympic Games in the summer of '96, and I hope to bring her brother Lance to the Olympic Games in 2000.

Acknowledgments

I'm a sports junkie, not an author. Or at least I *was* a sports junkie and not an author until I wrote this book. Now I guess I'm both. Several people deserve special recognition for their efforts in helping me add "writer" to my long list of interests.

John Perry, my editor, has been a welcome source of ideas for turning a recitation of events into a book aimed at sports fans, and one that appeals to a more general audience as well. He's non-partisan in the sports world and has undoubtedly been to more operas than to bowl games. His Oxford background and degrees in English and music counterbalance my Southern, sports-loving orientation. His creativity and imagination in labeling the episodes and sequencing the events will make the reader's journey much more entertaining.

Thanks also go to Greg Wilbur and Ginny Elder for their help in translating my doctor's handwriting into something legible that John could apply his magic craft to.

And to all those fathers and sons who seek to build their fellowship and create those wonderful memories by attending sporting events together, I say thank you most of all.

Foreword

Imagine yourself sitting on the fifty-yard line at the mythical National College Football Championship. Unbelievable. What about attending four major football bowl games in one week? Impossible. A prime spot at the opening ceremonies of the Olympic Games? Don't even think about it.

Yet Jack Newcomb is living proof it all can be done. Not by millionaire fat cats with connections. Not by captains of industry.

By *you*.

Jack has seen every famous sporting event you've ever heard of, and plenty that you haven't. The Super Bowl, the Olympics, Wimbledon, the World Series, and all the rest. But instead of relying on deep pockets and people in high places (neither of which he claims to have access to) Jack has counted on patience, skill, determination, luck, and a genuine love for sports to carry him through.

Every chapter in *The Ticket* represents an event Jack got in to see fair and square. No climbing over the fence, no watching from a hill outside the stadium. In a couple of situations he obviously had an inside track. But for each of those, many times he blazed a trail all by himself, methodically building one connection on top of another with nothing to fall back on but his enthusiasm.

Jack is not a wealthy man, but he spends wisely. You'll notice he often drives or carpools to events, or attends them when he's already in town on other business. He flies standby. He eats the free continental breakfast. True, if a friend offers him a ride on the company plane, he takes it. But in one exciting ticket quest after another, Jack demonstrates that you don't have to travel first class to have a lifetime of first-class memories.

Preface

Life is a journey. Live it to the fullest.That means you should get up off the couch and see, touch, taste, and smell all the world has to offer. And if you encounter a sporting event or two along the way, so much the better.

I have spent fifty years attending sporting contests all over the world. The most important thing I've learned is that there's no substitute for being there. The crowd noise, the tantalizing smell of hot dogs, the pizzas and pretzels, the weather, the local flavor, the crazy cab drivers, the chance sighting of a sports hero in a hotel lobby, and the attraction of the local sights — all work together to create an experience that the competition itself is only part of.

The bands, the music, the mascot, the stirring *Star Spangled Banner* are lost when you stay home and watch the game from the couch — no tailgate parties, no bantering with opposing fans, no sense of anticipation from the student for college athletics. Don't miss this excitement!

If God grants me old age, I don't want to spend it sitting in front of a television regretting I never saw it live when I had the health, the time, and the money. The ticket to a sporting event is also a ticket to live life to its fullest. I decided to write this book hoping to inspire you to become part of this action.

Another reason for writing is that our world is desperately short of heroes. We have plenty of celebrities. But heroes are another critter entirely. A sports ticket is, occasionally, a key to see real heroes in person. It also makes a father or mother into a hero in the eyes of a child who gets to share a sporting experience with them. "See a hero; sit with one too."

In fact, my lifelong quest for The Ticket began with my birthday present in 1946, tickets to see a football game with my dad in Knoxville between the University of Tennessee and the University of North Carolina. That was prime time for us, and the game was only part of the joy of being together. I was receptive to advice I might have stiff-armed any other time of the week. We had each other's undivided attention. It's the best bridge I know for spanning the communications gap. And you'll both remember the time together as long as you live. The Ticket is a ticket to life's memory machine.

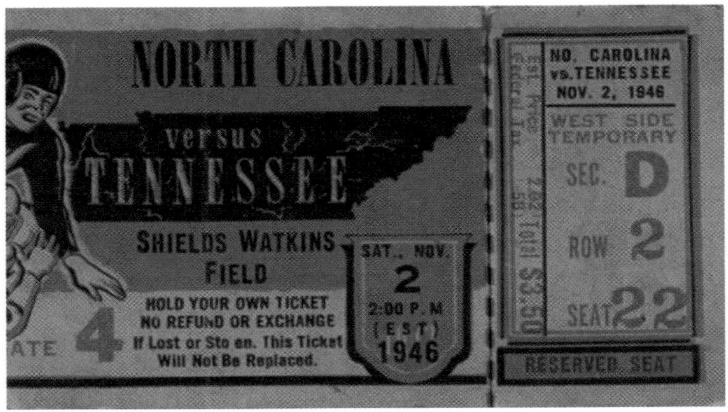

A final reason for spending the first year-and-a-half of my retirement scratching on a legal pad and poking at a word processor is to pass along the tips I've picked up all these years. How do you get tickets to impossible events? With very few exceptions, all it takes is tenacity and a spirit of adventure. You'll benefit from being there in person, and so will the athletes. "Your teams need your support." Athletes perform at their peak when the seats are full and the fans are excited.

A total of 4,792 regular season professional team sports contests will be presented in America in 1997, plus thousands of college, amateur, and regional competitions, and thousands more contests in auto racing, tennis, golf, and other individual sports.

Go while you can.

Jack Newcomb
Nashville, Tennessee

Prologue

How It All Began

Coach Adolph Rupp's Fabulous Five were coming to Knoxville on January 22, 1949. Having won the 1948 NCAA championship, this basketball team was hailed as the greatest ever. Two All Americans, Alex Groza and Ralph Beard, wore the Kentucky royal blue. The others, Jim Line, Dale Barnstable, Cliff Barker, Walt Hirsch, and Wah-Wah Jones, took a back seat to no one, including their more-heralded teammates.

Seeing this team, this coach, this budding tradition in person became a dream for every boy in the South who loved basketball. (In person, after all, was the only way we could see it. Television was something rich people in New York had, and Tennessee's first station was still a year away.) A twelve-year-old Tennessee Volunteer fan would never betray his loyalty in this match-up, uneven as it would be, but I was dying to see Coach Rupp's team. My dad agreed to make the trip to Knoxville, though I don't know whether my entreaties convinced him to go, or whether he was as excited as I was about seeing the Wildcats invade our home court.

The weather for the drive to the game was questionable, and the hour-long trip eastward from Harriman, Tennessee, to Knoxville began with snow flurries. After arriving at Alumni Memorial Gymnasium on the Tennessee campus, we walked unassumingly up to the ticket window. Before my dad could open his mouth, the gum-chewing lady at the window was already shaking her head.

"Sorry, sold out. No tickets." And you could tell from looking at her, that was the end of it.

The gymnasium — the label used before field houses, armories, arenas, super domes, and other glitzy handles came into fashion — seated approximately 3,300. As we stood outside in the cold watching all the fans with overcoats and felt hats enter with their tickets, my enthusiasm, built up over days in anticipation of the big game, fizzled in a heartbeat. What will we do?

The thought had never entered my trusting, optimistic mind that I would not see the Fabulous Five.

I don't remember if my dad asked anyone if they had any extra tickets or not. I was outside, and my dream was inside, about to begin without me. We stood shifting our weight in the lightly falling snow, watching helplessly as people holding those precious tickets paraded in front of us. When the last fans entered and those double doors closed, we retraced our steps back to the parking lot for the long drive westward and home.

Next morning, I pawed past the Sunday funnies to the sports section. My Volunteers had struggled valiantly in a 66-51 loss, and I had missed it for lack of a $1.50 ticket. Closing those doors on that small childhood dream marked the beginning of a lifetime of sports fulfillment. I have never been shut out since. And if I have extra tickets, and see a man and his boy looking for tickets, I pass the dream along.

Of more than eight-hundred sporting events I've attended since, this book tells the stories, experiences, and the fun of the best of them during my fifty-year chase for The Ticket.

Whetting the Appetite

All-Star Game — 1951, '53, '87

The Glory That Was Baseball

Imagine the excitement of a fourteen-year-old boy who's about to see baseball's greatest — Ted Williams, Joe Di Maggio, Enos Slaughter, Ralph Kiner, Jackie Robinson, Stan Musial, Duke Snider, Robin Roberts, George Kell. The year was 1951; the place was Briggs Stadium in Detroit, and my dad and I were boarding the train to see these future Hall-of-Famers play. Eighteen played that day!

Getting tickets had been as easy as a handwritten request to the Detroit Tigers office. When they arrived by return mail, I had to show them to my neighborhood buddies. As far as I knew, no one from Harriman, Tennessee, had ever been to the All-Star Game. Some of the guys were for the Yankees; others rooted for the Indians, the Red Sox, Dodgers, Cardinals, and Reds. I was the only Tiger fan. Each of us had our own reason for pulling for our chosen team, usually a favorite player. One of those All-Stars drove your decision.

Prices are at their peak in the hour or two before an event when the crowd starts pouring in. Prices usually drop — sometimes dramatically — as game time approaches. Stand-offs between buyers and sellers often continue after the start of the game. Don't be surprised that someone with extra tickets will hold out for their asking price after the game is underway, occasionally taking the extra tickets into the game with them.

My loyalty came from seeing the Tigers play the Yankees in a 1948 home game. That 1-0 contest planted a daily habit during baseball season that's carried through until today: checking the box score. I had to know if George Kell had any hits, and then see what Ted Williams did. Those two battled for the batting title back and forth through the early '50s until Williams left to fly with the Marines in the Korean War.

The guys and I followed our individual heroes as much as we did our favorite teams, and the chance to see so many of my players at once was part of the excitement. Three Tigers were in the action. George Kell would cover the corner at third base; Vic Wertz was slated for right field, and Freddie Hutchinson would pitch three innings. Each player would be wearing their team's uniform, The American League in home white and The National League in the road gray.

The last time the All-Star game had been played in Detroit, in 1941, Ted Williams was the big story. That hit, he said later, was the biggest thrill of his career — into the right field upper deck in the bottom of the ninth. Three runs scored and the AL won 7-5.

My dad and I got to the stadium and found our seats. Who cared that we sat in the lower left field deck? I was there, breathing the same air as the greatest stars in baseball! Looking over toward the dugouts and behind the plate, I saw the season ticket holders and dignitaries in their summer seersucker and straw hats. Very important people. They were supposed to be in those seats. Vernor's Ginger Ale came from Detroit. I figured the Vernor's people could probably get seats like that.

We watched the American League go down in defeat 8-3. But what could be more exciting than six home runs? Bob Elliott, Stan Musial, Gil Hodges, and Ralph Kiner hit the four-baggers for the National League and George Kell and Vic Wertz thrilled the hometown crowd with their homers.

Two years later, the Cincinnati Reds hosted the All-Star game at old Crosley Field. Since it was only half as far as Detroit, and dad and I could ride the Southern Railroad to Cincinnati, surely he would take me again. Baseball was my dad's favorite sport, so it didn't take too much convincing. Again, all a boy had to do was order tickets and they'd be sent by return mail. Even if the game sold out, that never happened until almost game day. No certified check, no registered mail, no ticket lottery. I probably mailed them cash.

Cincinnati fans had voted heavily for their hometown heroes, so the 1953 All-Star game had a strong showing of Reds on the National League team. During this stretch, the American League teams were winning the World Series and the National League was winning the All-Star games. The Yankees were on their way to a fifth straight American League pennant — a record — and a fifth World Series Championship. Under the circumstances, I guess Casey Stengel, the Yankees manager, couldn't get too worked up about his All-Star team losing one game in the middle of the season. The National League did it again, 5-1.

My fascination with the All-Star baseball game had long passed by 1987, but by then I had entered the phase in my life (still in it) when the challenge of getting a tough ticket got my competitive juices flowing. I was in San Francisco at the American Trial Lawyers'

Association annual meeting. Whether I knew the All-Star game would be played across the bay in Oakland that week, I don't remember. However, I was in town; the All-Star game was beckoning; and a person can sit through only so many hours of legal ego-building. An afternoon at the ballpark sounded like a perfect escape.

If you're taking your wife to San Francisco for a week in July, a baseball game in Oakland is probably not on her short list. Sonoma, Napa Valley, the Golden Gate Bridge, the Victorian mansions, China Town, otters at the Cliff House, lunch across the bay at Sausalito, Fisherman's Wharf, a stroll through the Fairmont, and shopping — all are likely to take priority.

I traveled alone. The BART ran from downtown San Francisco right to the Oakland Stadium. Lots of folks were looking for tickets in the walkway from the platform to the park. Tickets were plentiful and overpriced. I opted to wait until game time. Prices usually drop, unless it is a real sell-out. Looking for a single helps. A fellow coming from a parking spot close to the stadium rushed from his car toward the gate. I say, "I need a single." "Yeah, I have one here." "How much?" "Face value." No haggling, no fuss, just a quick transaction.

I was in my seat in time to see the fly-bys before the game, an SR-71 Blackbird, gargantuan C-5, and a formation of fighters. The SR-71 from Beale AFB about 125 miles northeast of Oakland made an impressive low-level flight over the stands. At that altitude and appearing suddenly overhead it caused a shudder through the crowd.

The airplanes turned out to be the biggest excitement of the day. The game was really lackluster. Maybe millionaire players couldn't create the same excitement as my heroes did that Tuesday in Detroit thirty-six years before. Maybe I had seen too many Final Fours, Masters, and thrilling football games. Those other competitions generate their own brand of adrenaline-charged action, but baseball is not a quick fix, not a pill to take if you're in the mood for immediate excitement. Basketball does that for a crowd, with its non-stop action. Baseball is like a sunset, or a seashore, or a mountain top — you need to sit and soak the total ambiance. Get the feel for the moment; enjoy the pleasure of being unrushed. Detroit had it. Cincinnati had it. I'll always be glad my dad shared it with me.

To grab all the gusto from baseball, sunsets, seashores or mountaintops, you need to be with someone you love. Sharing the experience makes it all the more enjoyable. Dads and husbands, take note!

Sugar Bowl 1957

Burned biscuits make sweet memories

An undefeated University of Tennessee team would play Baylor University on January 1, 1957, in the Sugar Bowl. All American Johnny Majors had just finished as runner-up to Paul Hornug in the Heisman Trophy competition. UT was 10-0 and Notre Dame was 2-8, but the team results failed to influence that cherished college trophy. UT Coach Bowden Wyatt was named Coach of the Year.

As a UT student, getting a ticket was no problem. Traveling to New Orleans was another matter. In today's world getting there would be a simple matter for a twenty-year-old. You'd get two or three buddies, pile in somebody's car, and drive 650 miles on the interstate. But in 1957, none of us owned a car. It was either a bus, the train, or hook a ride with adults who would be driving.

I could ride the train on my dad's railroad pass, since my name was on it too. My buddies, Ted Britt and Bill Charles Wright, opted

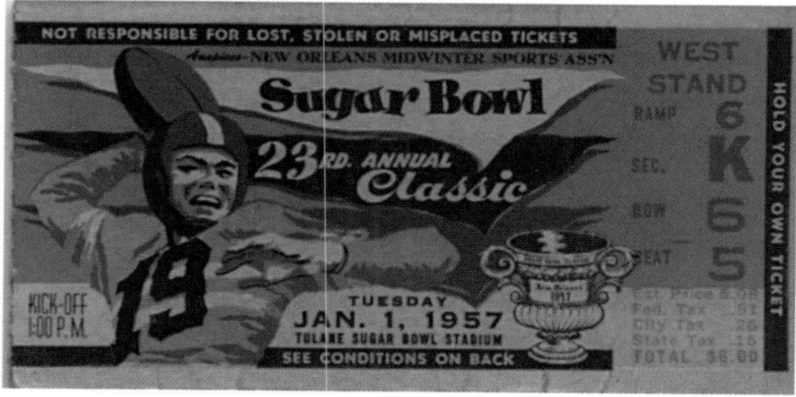

for the bus. I would meet them at our run-down hotel off Canal Street across from the French Quarter. We'd share the same room to cut costs, a hallowed student tradition that continues to this day, I assume.

Our first New Year's Eve in New Orleans was an eye opener. All the fans partying in the French Quarter exceeded anything that we had ever seen at a college football game, or anywhere else for that matter. We dutifully visited Pat O'Brien's and all it had to offer. To this day I have vivid memories of the lanky black man who accompanied the piano music by playing nickels on a silver tray with his thimbled fingers. He was still playing at the SEC basketball tournament in 1996.

Baylor upset the Vols that day, 13-7. A misty, dreary day added to the disappointing outcome of my first visit to a major bowl game. Even Johnny Majors' fumble of a Baylor punt could not overshadow his brilliant All-American career in his final football game. As his mother remarked, "Even the best of cooks burn the biscuits every once in awhile." Whether Tennessee could have been National Champions over Oklahoma is one of those subjective questions that stoked controversy for years to follow.

The train ride home on January 2 has been the source of one of my oft-told stories. As my dad's train pass expired on December 31, 1956, and he had not received his 1957 pass when I left for New Orleans, I had to do some contingency planning. (I was unfamiliar with that phrase then, but learned of it later in the military.) Before leaving East Tennessee on December 29, I purchased a one-way ticket from New Orleans to Oakdale, Tennessee, as a back-up. Lots of Tennessee fans boarded *The Southern Crescent* for the overnight trip back to Tennessee. When the conductor came through punching tickets, I presented him with my expired train pass, to which he said, "Son, this pass has expired." I explained, "But my dad hadn't received his new pass when I left home to come to the Sugar Bowl."

Somewhat in exasperation and somewhat in sympathy, the nice old gentleman said, "They always leave these things up to the conductor." He handed my pass back and inserted the small ticket stub atop the seat that indicated how far I was traveling. With that, I relaxed for the remainder of the trip. When my mother picked me up at the Oakdale depot I asked her to wait a minute. The ticket agent happily refunded my one-way ticket. The kind conductor probably felt that our losing to Baylor was enough bad luck for one trip. Throwing me off the train would have been just too much to, uh, bear.

Sugar Bowl — 1986

Inside the Big Orange

Early Saturday morning before the University of Tennessee/ Vanderbilt game in 1985, the phone rang at my Uncle Howard's home in Knoxville where Ginger and I were visiting. A win that day would place UT in the Sugar Bowl as the SEC host team. The call was from Dr. Fred Killiffer, a lifelong friend and one of the UT team doctors, inviting me to the UT locker room before and after the game. Though I'd been a UT fan all my life, I'd never seen the pregame festivities from the inside. What a treat!

Such a special occasion required a wardrobe to match. Making an appearance in the Tennessee locker room in a plain vanilla jacket was absolutely out of the question. My wife, Ginger, drove me by the UT bookstore, home of the largest collection of orange paraphernalia in the world, possibly in the universe. Wearing my new Big Orange jacket, I exited the student center and strutted in fine form to the stadium.

Be nice to your high school buddies. You never know who they'll turn out to be.

Kiff (the nickname we put on the future Dr. Killiffer while still in high school) met me at the entrance gate at the north end of the stadium and led the way to the locker room. The mood was surprisingly subdued and businesslike. Since this was the final home game, tradition called for the seniors to be introduced individually, shake hands with Coach Majors, and then run through a giant "T" formed by the band. As I stood there at the north end zone, not ten feet away, I watched each of these young men receive Coach Majors' thanks and race through

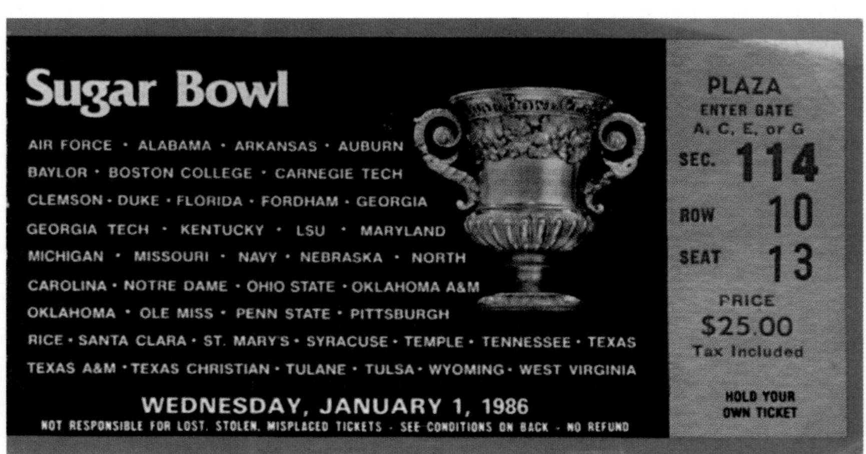

the "T" to the applause of 94,000-plus fans. This old UT fan relished every second of those players' last moment of glory on this field. Imagine what they felt like. I'm surprised they didn't pop their pads off.

At the end of the pre-game warm-up, Kiff told me to come back to the locker room after the game. The Vols defeated Vanderbilt 30-0 and were on their way to the Sugar Bowl. I was waiting at the goal posts by the north end when the team carried Coach Majors off the field. I can still see his huge grin as they came through the tunnel. (I saw that grin six years later, after an amazing come-from-behind win in South Bend in 1991. That day Tennessee beat the Irish 35-34.)

Back in the locker room the enthusiasm quieted when Mr. Mickey Holmes stood and extended the Sugar Bowl Committee's official invitation to the SEC Champions, the University of Tennessee Volunteers. Then the room erupted. Tennessee was back in the Sugar Bowl for the first time in fifteen years.

Sugar Bowl or not, New Orleans means food. That evening I telephoned three restaurants there for reservations over the New Year holiday: the Commanders' Palace, Jonathan's, and Le Ruth's. Out of all the legendary restaurants in New Orleans, at that time only one was five-star, and that was Le Ruth's in Gretna. Restaurant reservations concerned me more than hotel reservations. When they were safely made, it was only a matter of when to drive down.

We arrived in the Crescent City four nights before the Sugar Bowl, earlier than I had ever been for a bowl game. Ginger and I had picnics in the parks, toured the old plantation mansions along Magnolia Alley, visited the Garden District and the Zoo, and mingled with the 18,000 fans who had followed UT for this meeting with the favored University of Miami.

On the evening of the game, we scheduled a rendezvous with my good friend Fletch Lowe, now departed, and some of his air crew. After we met at Felix's Oyster Bar, his favorite New Orleans hangout, Fletch challenged me by asking, "Newcomb, have you ever been to two bowl games in one season?" He knew of my sporting events addiction and figured he had put me in a "check" position. I had in fact attended the Gator Bowl between UT and Florida in December of 1969, and then motored on to Miami for the Penn State-Missouri Orange Bowl game on New Year's Day, 1970.

Since he was about to tie my feat, he had thrown down the gauntlet! (At that moment, Fletch inspired me to take one of my all-time great trips: four bowls in seven days in three states. More on that later.)

Sugar Bowl tickets were as common as crawfish. On the way from the Hyatt Hotel to the Superdome, I saw people swapping tickets for cups of beer. At least they were big cups. I had ordered my tickets through the University of Tennessee Athletic Department and had lousy seats in the upper deck end zone. So I did some trading, and ended up in the Miami section at mid-field, in the lower deck ten rows back.

At the outset the Hurricane fans were riding me awfully hard. I wore a UT baseball cap, and their team took the early lead by returning the opening kick-off and scoring behind Vinny Testaverde. The Vols' #1 quarterback had gone out with a knee injury in the fifth game of the season, against Alabama. Daryl Dickey, the replacement QB, had led them through the balance of the year unbeaten, but he was no Tony Robinson, especially when it came to passing. That night though, the defense swarmed Testaverde and created five turnovers. The little Miami ladies who sat behind me screaming long and loudly during the first quarter were a lot quieter by the end of the first half. By the third quarter, they were nowhere to be seen.

Tennessee fans can be loud. Some say obnoxious, some say intolerable. But the Superdome amplified the cheers beyond anything I ever heard before or since. It hurt my ears, but a 35-7 victory was worth every decibel. After the win, the Felix's Oyster Bar crowd reconvened to replay one of the most memorable and enjoyable games in UT football history.

My friends who watched the game on TV told me later that Keith Jackson had pronounced the game's inevitable outcome after Miami took an early 7-0 lead. Ray Broyles, the color commentator, predicted that UT's defense could never contain Vinny Testaverde. But they didn't know what was inside the Big Orange!

On January 2 we left five days of New Orleans memories and food fests behind and headed for home. After all those fancy dinners in the Mecca of Fine Dining, I could hardly wait for some plain, rough grub. We pulled off the interstate in Hattiesburg, Mississippi, and drove to the campus of Southern Mississippi University in search of a hamburger joint. I wanted the fattest, greasiest, most overloaded hamburger I could put my mouth around, and a thick milk shake. After my "Grease Level Low" light was out at last, I continued my transition back to the real world.

Little did I imagine all the great sporting events that would come my way in the balance of 1986. This Sugar Bowl trip was the first of thirty-two sporting events for me over the next twelve months!

Final Four — 1966

The night they drove Old Dixie down

People who know of my love for sports and the thrill of the chase will eventually get around to the inevitable question. "Which is your favorite event?" The fact that I've been to eleven Final Fours is a dead give-away. Basketball is where my life as a fan and die-hard ticket detective began, being turned away from that Tennessee-Kentucky basketball game in 1949 (which would have been my first taste of college basketball). For my money, the Final Four is the most exciting contest in sports.

My enthusiasm for this series has continued to grow through the years, in a large part because of the way basketball tournaments work. Win today or you're out. No second chances. For me, that adds to the attraction. Of course, CBS has certainly done their part with a long-standing TV contract and their ever-increasing hype of the "Road to the Final Four."

The Final Four and The Masters (my two favorites) are usually

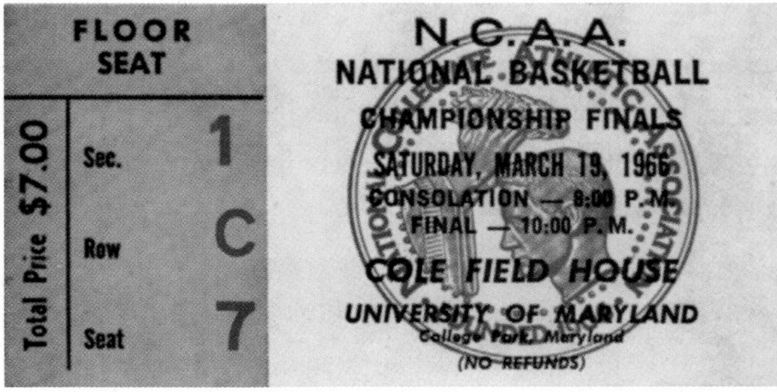

played on consecutive weekends, and probably represent the two toughest tickets to obtain in sports. Logistically it's a tall order to attend both in the same year, but in 1966, '85, '86, '88, and '93 I managed to pull it off. (For the years 1966 and 1988 scheduling permitted me to include the baseball Opening Day game as well.) More about all that later on.

One of the most exciting and far-reaching Final Fours of all time was the one recalled by an article in the April 1, 1991, issue of *Sports Illustrated* entitled "The Night They Drove Old Dixie Down." That issue marked the twenty-fifth anniversary of the biggest upset in Final Four history: Texas Western defeating Coach Adolph Rupp's awesome Kentucky team. Coach Don Hoskins' all-black team surprised the all-white Wildcats, a team composed of Pat Riley, Louie Dampier, Tommy Kron, Thad Jararez, and Larry Conley. (The photograph below, paid permission of Rich Clarkson & Associates, shows my wife and me standing behind the Kentucky bench during the awards presentations after the game.)

Although I saw that contest, one of the most intriguing facts about it would remain a secret for 29 years.

The '66 championship changed college basketball forever. UCLA had won NCAA titles in 1964 and 1965, and in 1967 would begin an unprecedented seven-year reign as champs. In 1966, Coach John Wooden played second fiddle to Coach Rupp in terms of national championships, wins, esteem, and overall acclaim. Time and victories would ultimately change that perception in the world of college basketball. But in '66, Coach Rupp was seeking an unprecedented fifth NCAA title. At that time such an accomplishment was as unthinkable and unattainable as five U.S. Open golf championships, or any other wild dream. Coach Rupp wanted win number five desperately. He had won in 1948, '49, '51, and 1958. He had never gone more than eight years without a title.

Believe it or not, tickets to the 1966 Final Four were still a relatively easy buy, compared with today's feeding frenzy. (Tickets to see the Beatles in Shea Stadium that year would probably have been a lot tougher. I wouldn't know.) Though fans created a healthy demand for tickets, my boss at the time, Lt. Col. Robert Stroop, was able to get me a pair. He knew of my addiction to sports, and his older son played baseball for the University of Maryland, the Final Four host school. A certain allocation of tickets was available to that school, a practice that continues today. (Colonel Stroop is the tall gentleman behind me in the Kentucky bench photograph.)

At that time the Final Four games were played on Friday and Saturday nights. Duke and Utah joined Texas Western and Kentucky in the competition. It was widely assumed that the winner of the UK/Duke game in the semifinals on Friday night would eventually be the national champions.

My wife-to-be did not appreciate Coach Rupp's dominance of basketball, nor did she share my zeal for Wildcat basketball. Since her roommate was dating an All-American guard on the Duke team, Bob Verga, and we had been to see him play in the aging Cameron Indoor Stadium, her heart was with Duke, as she frequently reminded me.

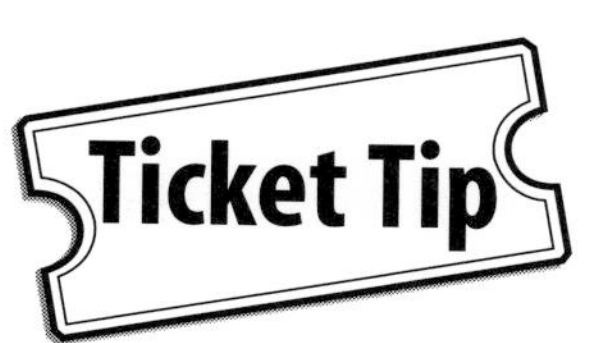

Check with friends who may have attended the host school. And ask around — you never know what friend or co-worker might be an alumnus or have a relative attending there.

Friday was a typical run-and-gun Kentucky game. It was in fact a fantastic ballgame, a classic Final Four shoot-out. We sat in Section 1, Row C behind the basket, at that time my favorite place to see a basketball game. There was little space between the goal and the seats at Maryland's Cole Fieldhouse, or in any of the fieldhouses of that pre-dome era. Those seats put you close to the basket, and nearer to the action than mid-court, when basketball was still basically a non-contact sport, quite different from the way it's played today. It was also a time when fans dressed up for the games, and smoking was part of the experience and the ambiance. Ergo, I wore a dark blue suit in support of Kentucky and smoked my prized cigar. With the close score, fast breaks, and exciting action on the part of the 'Cats and the Blue Devils, I was up and down in my seat during the entire game on Friday, rooting Kentucky on to a 83-79 win.

At Saturday night's finals, a different fellow was in the seat next to me. As I was confident of a Wildcat victory, and the consolation games were never of any real consequence, I was a bit calmer at the start of the game. During the course of our conversation, I asked my new seat-mate what happened to the fan from the night before. He took some delight in telling me that his friend had asked him to exchange seats with him for the Finals. His friend had described my reprehensible enthusiasm for Kentucky basketball and preferred to swap seats. I think the new occupant sat there more to see my hysterical game antics than as a favor to his buddy. The way it turned out, the other fan would have had nothing to worry about. With Kentucky trailing and eventually losing in the Championship game, I had much less reason to be excited.

Now, fast forward twenty-nine years, to Easter Sunday at a Presbyterian church in Salt Lake City. After the service, I wandered into the fellowship hall for a cup of coffee while my wife, daughter, and son-in-law went to retrieve the grandchildren from the pre-school class. The church members wore name tags, and I noticed an older gentleman wearing the name Jack Gardner. My interest piqued, I approached him to ask, "Are you Coach Gardner that coached at the University of Utah?" In a very humble, polite, and unassuming manner he confirmed my hunch. Here was a kind, elderly church member no one paid any special attention to. But I had just found a member of the Basketball Hall of Fame who was a walking history of the sport.

Having come from the '95 Final Four in Seattle earlier in the week, my memory was refreshed on NCAA history. I had worked at being able to recite all the Final Four championships, so I remembered that Utah had won in 1944. While that had been fifty-one years prior, I still had to ask him if he had coached that 1944 championship team. I think he realized any Nashvillian who knew Utah won the 1944 NCAA basketball title was a serious fan. I believe I established a little credibility.

He was not their head coach in 1944, but he went on to say that he was the only person to have attended every Final Four dating back to Oregon's win in 1939. He was also the only coach to take two different teams twice each to the Final Four: Kansas State and Utah.

Sometime during this exchange, my wife gave my sleeve a discreet tug, indicating it was time to leave. I introduced her to Coach Gardner and said I wanted to stay and talk. You don't meet history on the hoof every day. After she left, I mentioned the NCAA picture of the '66 Finals, and that it had been her first Final Four. With that, he told me "the rest of the story" of Texas Western and Coach Hoskins.

Prior to the 1965-66 basketball season, Coach Hoskins had contacted Coach Gardner to ask about some coaching assistance, a sort of an informal mini-clinic. Coach Gardner's team had a reputation for a great fast-break offense, and Hoskins wanted to learn more about his approach, tactics, and methods. So Coach Gardner made practice film and game film available to him. Gardner told me that by the end of the process, "Coach Hoskins knew more about my team than I did." Little did Coach Gardner know that his generosity would be his undoing in the semifinals of the 1966 Final Four! Texas Western defeated Coach Gardner's Utah team 85-78.

That was Coach Gardner's last coaching visit to the Final Four. But after meeting this generous gentleman, I know he was never sorry to have shared his knowledge with others who love the game.

Jack Gardner is currently a consultant to the Utah Jazz team. Those who wonder how the Jazz pack the Delta Center for every home game probably attribute it to the Mailman Karl Malone, and Mr. Assist John Stockton. I believe it's the fact that Utah's basketball roots go back to the 1944 NCAA Champions, and have been kept alive by a modest, unassuming genius named Jack Gardner. He was the secret weapon that put Texas Western in the spotlight "The Night They Drove Old Dixie Down," denying Coach Rupp an ever-elusive fifth NCAA title in his last visit to the Final Four.

Orange Bowl — 1966, '68, '69, '70, '72, '73

Ready for prime time, but not for the traffic

From the mid '60s to the mid '70s, the Orange Bowl was arguably the best of the bowl events. In those years, the Orange Bowl committee made a real effort to match up the two best teams in the country, at least those that didn't already have a commitment with a conference alliance, and give us football fans the closest thing possible to a national college championship.

One of the most important contributions the Orange Bowl made to the football bowl season was in going from the traditional afternoon kick-off to TV prime time. Since all the other bowls were over by then, this meeting of two ranked powers in Miami had an added sense of finality and drama, especially when a number-

one ranked team was playing. Having the game under the lights made for a sensational halftime extravaganza, especially for the live crowd, though the TV audience got a taste of it. In 1996 for the first time the Bowl Alliance matched the Number One and Number Two non-Rose Bowl teams for the national title. If, after thirty years, the bowl games have finally moved toward a play-off system, I credit the Orange Bowl for being the first to try to bring the two best, highest ranked teams together and settle the score on the field, instead of some subjective poll.

My run of six Orange Bowls found the following match-ups.

1966	Alabama	39	Nebraska	28
1968	Oklahoma	26	Tennessee	24
1969	Penn State	15	Kansas	14
1970	Penn State	10	Missouri	3
1972	Nebraska	38	Alabama	6
1973	Nebraska	40	Notre Dame	6

All those games were complete sell-outs prior to the game. But, as with each of the eighteen bowl games I've attended (except for the Penn State-Miami game in 1987, when those teams played for the National Championship), tickets were easy to get.

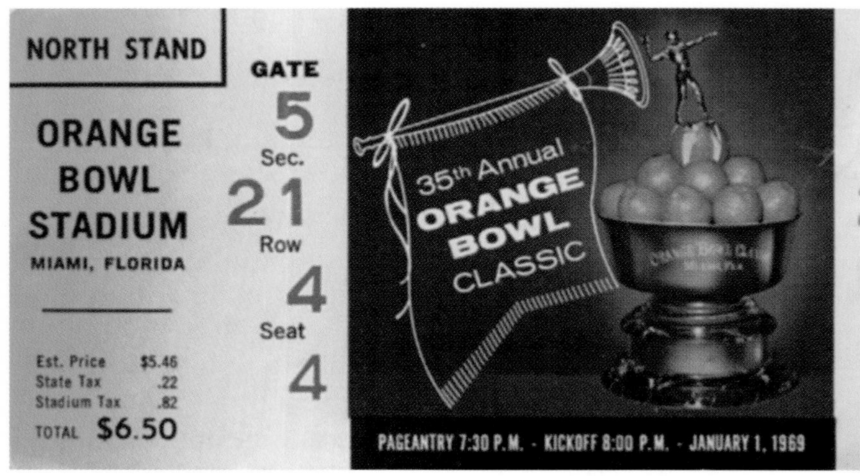

Participating teams typically receive about 15,000 tickets per school, usually from the twenty-yard lines back toward the goal and wrapping around into their respective end zones. Corporate sponsors and the locals usually sweep up the cream of the crop. The good news for ticket hounds is that, unless it is a Number One/Number Two match-up, the demand falls off for those prime tickets as game day approaches. In those days, fans traveling from a Big Eight school would bring more extra tickets with them than there were fans traveling that far without a ticket. In short, even for the most popular bowl games, you'll usually discover that a hotel room will be harder to find than a ticket.

In fact, before my last two bowl trips, the Hall of Fame Bowl in 1993 and the Gator Bowl in 1995, I didn't even bother responding to the bowl ticket applications mailed to season ticket holders after the bowl announcements. You can shop around at the bowl city or at the game and get better seats than you can order through the mail, so why buy tickets in advance? Took me sixteen bowl games to figure that out. The bowl alliance may change that, but it should make a real difference only in the Number One and Number Two match-up.

Another good course of action is to identify notable alums who don't travel to bowl games. At big football schools, the larger your annual contribution or charitable remainder trust bequest, the better your seat. However, some large contributors do not follow their team to the bowl games or on the road. These ticket holders are an excellent source for premium seats.

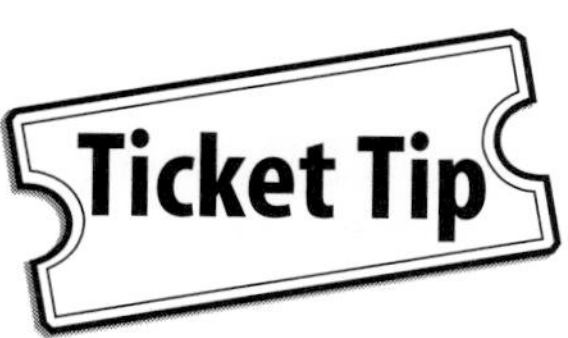

Bowl tickets at the game are usually better than what you can order by mail. The downside is that you may have to sit with the enemy.

Of course, if you're the kind of votary who doesn't like surprises, or you feel better sitting in your team's section, you should order tickets through your university.

I began to apply my new-found understanding of bowl ticket supply and demand during my fourth Orange Bowl trip, in 1970. That was my first year to complete a double header, two bowl trips in one season. The University of Tennessee had completed a 9-and-2 season and was meeting Florida in the Gator Bowl on December 27. That year, on my way to my annual Florida visit with good friend Don Ballew and his family, I stopped in Jacksonville to see the Gator

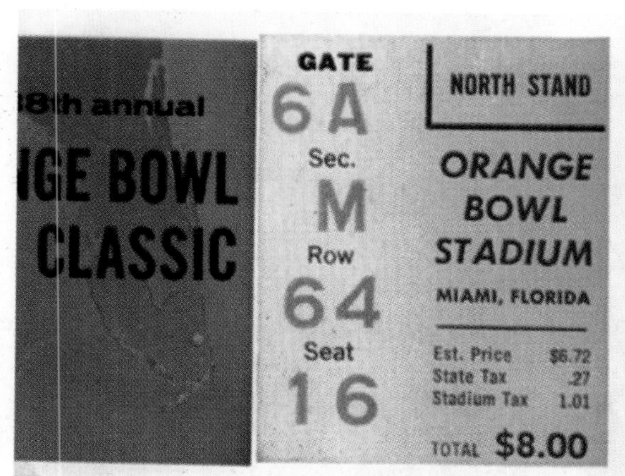

Watch for school colors on your way to the game. You'll likely find many promising ticket sources. "Tickets Needed" signs in your car window will produce results.

Bowl. I'd ordered tickets through the UT Athletic Department. Florida won that game 14-13. The irony of the defeat was the resignation of UT Coach Doug Dickey immediately after the game. His new head coaching job was with his alma mater — the University of Florida!

Somewhat dismayed by that double loss, we continued on to the Ballews. Penn State was playing Missouri in the Orange Bowl that year. On the way down I-95 from Jacksonville, if I saw Penn State colors or Missouri fans, I checked with them for extra tickets. I was holding out for good seats, not just two tickets. You never know what you'll uncover just by asking. That game turned out to be another close contest, with Penn State winning 10-3.

The 1970 Orange Bowl taught me a valuable lesson the hard way. My friends Don Ballew and Paul Daly, both Dolphins season ticket holders, always came up with good seats at face value for the

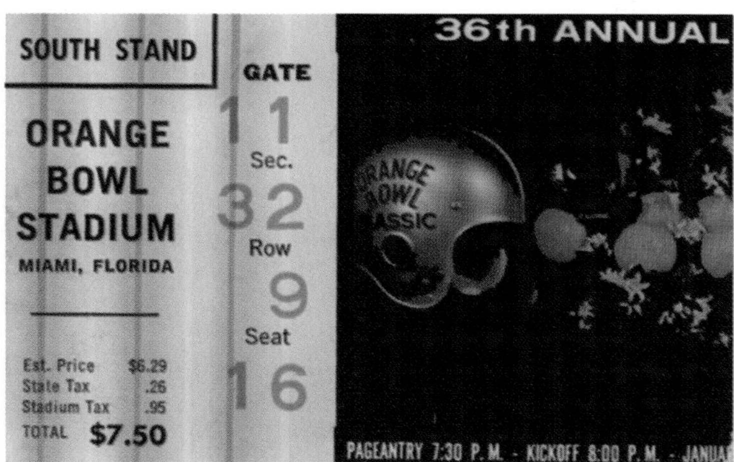

Orange Bowl, and the '70 contest was no exception. The game that year lacked the offensive punch and excitement we had savored in our earlier Orange Bowl visits. During the fourth quarter, with the score tied seemingly forever at 3-3, Don said, "Let's go and beat the traffic." I have never been able to understand the logic of leaving a game early. Why go to a game unless you are going to see who wins? But in deference to my host's wishes, I left. While we were walking to the car, a huge roar came from the stadium. I couldn't believe it! "Ballew," I said, "Someone just scored and we're out here. We sat through three-and-a-half quarters and don't even know who won the game." I let him have it for the balance of my stay. Since that day, one of my few hard and fast rules is that I do not leave games early. And on sporting trips I've taken with Don since, I've been known to ask, especially in a close game, "Hey, do you want to beat the traffic?"

Preakness — 1965,'66, '67

The age of elegance

Before the mid '60s, lack of fan interest in sporting events meant many of the majors didn't sell out. Such was the case of the Preakness, the middle gem in the Triple Crown. Then as now, the Kentucky Derby garnered most of the notoriety in thoroughbred racing. The Preakness, the shortest Triple Crown race at 1 3/16 mile, is born of the Maryland horse country tradition. The horse farms that dot the countryside there are evidence of a love of racing.

The Pimlico Race Course near Baltimore was founded in 1870, and it hosted the inaugural Preakness in 1873 (two years before Churchill Downs) under the auspices of Governor Oden Bowie and the President of the Maryland Jockey Club. It was still a grand place when I first visited there. For my three Preakness years, 1965, 1966, and 1967, we sat in the enclosed clubhouse, where costs were nominal and the view was excellent. My wife and I were joined by Earl

PIMLICO
RACE COURSE
SAT., MAY 15
1965 SPRING MEET
Est. Price $5.00
Fed. Tax 1.00
TOTAL $6.00
PREAKNESS
DAY
GRANDSTAND RESERVED SEAT
SECTION 6
ROW 1
SEAT 5
POSITIVELY NO REFUND

Ladd from Dallas, who had a regularly scheduled bank meeting in New York preceding the Preakness every year. (Good thinking, Earl!) After his meeting, Earl had stopped to see me in Washington, D.C., where we rehashed old times — the Boy Scout World Jamboree at Valley Forge in 1950, rooming together at Tennessee, and my visits with him when he lived in Queens, New York, including pre-dawn departures for golf on the Black Course at Bethpage Golf Course on Long Island.

The three of us enjoyed the class, the pace, the vista, and the ambiance of this racing jewel. I ordered tickets by mail several months in advance, directly from the Pimlico Track. In those years, choice clubhouse tickets would follow. (I still have the fancy straw hat I bought one year to complete my race day ensemble of flashy sport coat and black-and-white spectator shoes. I probably looked more like a racetrack hustler than a novice race fan.)

Today, Preakness tickets are in greater demand, despite the waning overall interest in thoroughbred racing. My more recent experiences with the industry convince me they're doing everything possible to bring horse fans back to the track. Racing management espe-

cially needs to cultivate the younger crowd. Otherwise, this spectacular sport may eventually be limited to those in the inner circles of the business and, to a lesser extent, the horse bettor. But with off-track betting facilities available today, the budding horse fan may ask, "Why spend a day at the track — with all the hassle of the crowd, parking, and admission — when a trip to the OTB arena or TV simulcast is so easy, and where the serious player can bet more races or even other sporting events?"

The Triple Crown makes my list of top sporting events as much for its tradition as for its stature in racing championships. It once drew the largest crowds of any sporting event and earned a reputation as the Sport of Kings. The Greek nobility rode to hounds, and history tells us they staged the first horse race between mounted riders in 642 B.C. In 1821, Union Race Course on Long Island became the first track to be enclosed by rails. In 1865, even before the last shots of the Civil War were exchanged, two New York sportsmen, John Hunter and William Travers, joined forces with John Morissey to found Saratoga, the oldest stakes race at the most picturesque racing oval in the country.

So many memories will stay just memories. The opportunities to revisit or to relive them are gone. Sports and venues change; friends come and go. But those one-time experiences are treasures forever.

American Odyssey

The Kentucky Derby — 1983

Horse trading

My trip to the Kentucky Derby began far from the twin towers and mint juleps of Churchill Downs. But it shows how a little horse trading can sometimes turn so-so tickets into something truly incredible.

It all started when I ordered four tickets to the NCAA Mid-East Regionals in Knoxville that year. At the time, team pairings for the tournament were still unknown, which meant getting tickets was completely routine. But when the schedule came out, the results were

a Kentucky basketball lover's dream: University of Louisville and University of Kentucky would go head to head for the first time in 24 years!

Suddenly the demand for tickets was enormous. Seeing a chance to attend the world-famous Kentucky Derby in style, I ran an ad in the Sunday *Courier-Journal* saying I would trade my basketball tickets for box seats to the Derby. When I came home from work the next day, my wife had taken over twenty-five calls. The offers included not only box seats, but also lodging for two nights, the Friday fillies race, parking for both days, and tickets for the Governor's Breakfast on Saturday morning! Now, among this embarrassment of riches, the question was which offer to accept.

After listening to Ginger's read on the various people who had called, I decided to split my tickets into two pairs and take two offers. One pair went to the caller with the best seats for the Derby (which he had kept in his safe deposit box) and the other to a father and his son, who was a member of the University of Louisville football team, in exchange for their basement apartment for the weekend, parking, and tickets to the fillies race on Saturday. At first I had a problem with spending the weekend in a total stranger's home, to which Ginger replied, "They sound like my kind of people."

Of course she was right. We arranged the great ticket swap at the Marriott on I-40 near the Nashville airport on the morning before the U of L/UK game. All parties were satisfied. Once again the Ticket Fairy had waved her magic wand.

I could hardly wait for Derby weekend, even with a forecast of rain. Our Friday parking spot was there as advertised; our hosts were delightful, and our box seats were under cover just past the finish line. Saturday began with rain and a sloppy track, but — who cared? I had a julep in my hand when an estimated 120,000 fans sang *My Old Kentucky Home*, and I was ready for the most famous horse race in the world.

My pre-race analysis of the racing form led me to put my money on Sonny's Halo. I don't recall the exact odds, but he was not the favorite, or even near the top. I decided to bet the largest wager I'd ever made — $50 across the board: $50 to win, $50 to place, and $50 to show. A hundred and fifty dollars on a horse race! But up to this point, I'd only invested the cost of four Mid-East Regional NCAA tickets in the whole enterprise, and here I was in box seats at Churchill Downs rubbing shoulders with all the celebs.

In the crowded men's room just before the Derby race, I noticed former Secretary of State Henry Kissinger. As he left the urinal, the man standing next to him said in a loud voice, "Wait until my wife hears who took a leak next to me!" Mr. Kissinger, by now at the wash basin, replied in his deep, eloquent bass voice, "Had I known the event would be so popular, I would have charged admission."

Back in my seat, pari-mutuel ticket stubs in hand, I was ready for what has rightly been called "the most exciting two minutes in sports." As the bell sounded, the horses left the starting gate to our left and thundered past on their way to the first turn, colors blazing, mud flying, with Sonny's Halo somewhere in the middle of the pack.

As if to end this remarkable adventure on an even more incredible note, Sonny's Halo crossed the finish line first a little over two minutes later. What a show! What had started with four tickets to a basketball game at Stokley Fieldhouse on the University of Tennessee campus had become a once-in-a-lifetime experience. Box seats, reserved parking, free accommodations, Henry Kissinger, and a winning horse. It just doesn't get any better.

World Series 1985

Thank you, Whitey Ford

When the Yankees played the first game of the 1961 World Series, I was stationed at McGuire Air Force Base in New Jersey. Whitey Ford would pitch the first game, and a couple of buddies and I who had been to several games together during the regular season agreed to drive to 161st Street in the Bronx for all the excitement at Yankee Stadium.

The morning of the game the weather was overcast, cool, and gloomy. And to my astonishment, my buddies faded on me. They decided to bag it, though I never knew whether it was on account of the weather or a late night at the Officer's Club.

Since I didn't think I'd enjoy going alone, I skipped the game, violating one of the Rules of Sport that I later adopted: Follow your urge to see the game, whether anybody wants to go or not. Whitey Ford pitched a shut-out that day against Cincinnati on his way to breaking Babe Ruth's World Series record for most consecutive scoreless innings in the Series. And I missed it! Whitey inspired me to make it to the Series one day, no matter what. But I had to wait 24 years for another chance.

Nashville, 1985. My good friend Buzz Davis and I walked onto the racquetball court at the downtown YMCA to play Jack Burch and Jimmy French in our regular doubles match. As we were warming up, Buzz turned to me suddenly and asked, "How would you like to go the World Series in St. Louis this week?"

"Whitey," I thought, "I'm finally going to make it." Though it was half a continent away from Yankee Stadium, and Whitey and his teammates were receding into sports history, I felt somehow the loop would be completed at last.

After an hour of fiery but friendly competition (where Buzz and I held our own against these two former Vanderbilt varsity athletes!), Buzz explained that we would be going on the Third National Bank airplane, which he had arranged to charter. Mr. and Mrs. Toby Wilt, friends of Baseball Commissioner Peter Ueberroth, had been invited to join the Commissioner in his box along the first base line for one of the games, and we could tag along on the company plane. But there was one catch: the rest of us had to come up with our own tickets. That was a challenge I took on with pleasure!

My wife, Ginger, and I met the other fans at Stevens Aviation for a 5:30 p.m. departure to the East St. Louis Airport. There we quickly boarded taxis to the Marriott Hotel downtown, where Toby and his

wife were to join the Commissioner for the evening's revelry. I didn't have a moment to lose. Buzz and Ginger were depending on me to be their Ticket Fairy. My preparation for this trek had included a trip to Third National Bank that afternoon for $600 in cash, my preliminary upper limit for a price on three tickets.

Set a price limit before you start looking for a ticket. It will keep you from paying more than you should, and drive you to use your best horse trading skills.

The ticket hawkers were present, but not plentiful. Since the first pitch was only a few minutes away, I had little time to compare prices or shop for the best seat locations. I bought two tickets down the right field line for $375, and suggested Buzz and Ginger take them while I continued the search. Buzz insisted that Ginger and I use the tickets. As the three of us walked toward the entrance, a single ticket appeared from a broker across the street. Another $150 and the three of use were in the door for our first World Series. The Cards took a lead but ultimately lost three straight in the I-70 Series against their cross-state rival, the Kansas City Royals.

After the game, we reconvened at the hotel lobby to wait on Mr. and Mrs. Wilt. Only later did we find out that we could have joined them and Commissioner Ueberroth for a post-game party in the Commissioner's suite! When Toby and Joanne returned from their whirlwind evening, we returned to Nashville, where I re-entered the real world for a night's sleep, or what was left of it, before another routine Thursday at work.

Had I gone on to Yankee Stadium 24 years earlier and purchased a $15 ticket to see Whitey Ford beat the Reds, would I have accepted Buzz Davis's offer to fly to St. Louis for a single World

Series game? Probably. The excitement of the game, and the thrill of tracking that unknown and elusive ticket, make it all worthwhile. As the fox hunter knows, the fun is in the chase.

But thanks anyway, Whitey. It's players like you that make us love the game.

Indianapolis 500 — 1986

Gentlemen, re-start your engines

As a flight attendant for Western Airlines at the time, my daughter was ever on the look-out for a ticket to any major sporting event for dear old dad. Since she was single then, as well as very attractive and personable, she met plenty of good-looking men who would strike up a conversation with her. One such young gentleman worked for CART, the Championship Auto Racing Team. He said he would be in Indianapolis for the week of the 500 race, and was willing to provide tickets for her. And her parents, of course.

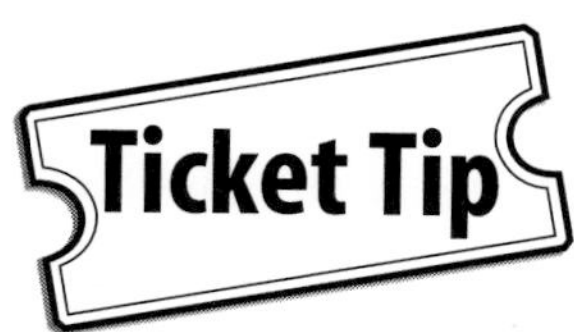

Few sporting events are postponed due to weather, but if one is, the rescheduling gives you a new shot at tickets. Some ticket holders won't be able to reschedule their trip. Be flexible and go for the re-start.

We didn't have much time. Indianapolis was close enough to drive from Nashville, but the hotel rooms for 150 miles had been booked since last year's Indy. I came up empty-handed in the search for decent accommodations. We finally took the next best thing, crummy accommodations.

A dreary motel couldn't dampen our enthusiasm. The parade, the tradition, the renovated Union Station, and all the fans in all the vans that lined the approach to the Speedway played a role in making this the best-attended single event in the world. The young guys had placed worn-out sofas on top of some of the vans to form a corridor of salutes to their older comrades passing by. Inside in the infield the youth continued their partying, including mud baths. We joined the 400,000 race fans streaming into the Brickyard, and made our way to the seats Morna's handsome passenger had produced.

About all you could say about the seats on this gray, drizzly day was that they were seats. From Section L in the third turn, we could have seen the speed of the cars on the back straight away, then watched them enter the third turn for the short stretch prior to making turn four. But all we saw that day were the preliminary events, including the motorcade with all the beautiful ladies perched on the backs of their convertibles. Top speed that day was probably 60 mph, since the racing cars, the real stars of the day, never left Gasoline Alley.

Chuck Yeager's day as Grand Marshal would be postponed. Rain and a wet track delayed the world-famous command, "Gentleman, start your engines," not only for that day, but for the whole week. It was only the second such delay in the seventy-five-year history of the race.

The following Friday, I joined Ray and Peggy Woodson at their table on Legislative Plaza in Nashville for a local charity breakfast. When the conversation turned to weekend plans, it turned out both of us were going to Indianapolis that evening. They were staying about one hundred miles south of Indianapolis and a second room was available there. With a better room (thank goodness!) and good friends for traveling companions, the prospects for the return trip seemed just as bright as the original.

The day of the rescheduled Indy 500 was bright and sunny, with blue skies and a slight cool bite in the air. As we approached the Speedway near the finish line, I noticed what seemed to be a buyer's market for tickets. I asked Ray to let me see about trading up on my seats. Success. I bought seats in Stand A, Box 14, between the finish line and the first turn — great for watching the line-up prior to the race, and with a grand view of Pit Row! From my new vantage point, I could see as well as hear the history-making commotion that begins with "Gentleman, start your engines." Three hours later Bobby Rahal took the checkered flag.

Eight years and several NASCAR outings afterward, Ray and I would be in the adjoining stand for the inaugural 400 race with the NASCAR boys at the Brickyard. But that's another story.

NBA Finals — 1986

Houston honcho

The Houston Rockets were hosting the Boston Celtics in game five of the 1986 NBA finals. At that time, Houston was one of the closest NBA team cities with a direct flight from my home in Nashville. With that kind of action so close, I had to give Southwest Airlines a call, just in case. Lo and behold, they ran an inexpensive flight into Hobby Field, and seating was available. I'd never been to an NBA championship, and it was time to fill that missing square. A late afternoon flight had me in Houston by 5:30 p.m. Now to get a ticket.

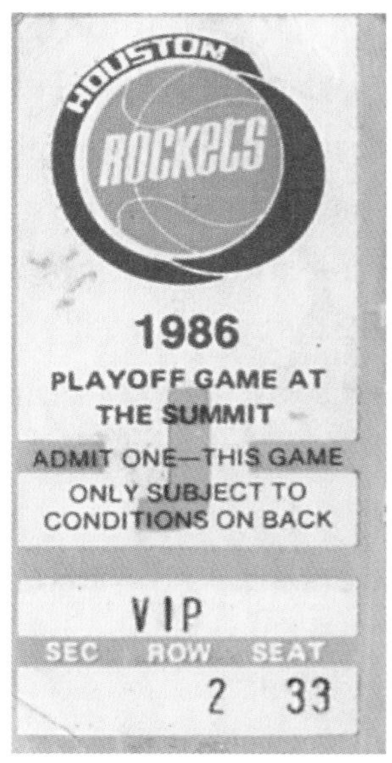

Riding to the hotel across from the Summit arena, I recognized a fellow from previous sporting events. He was a handsome young man, probably early 30s, who had hawked tickets at the Final Four in Lexington. My wife and I had chatted with him briefly in the lobby of the Hyatt Hotel that day in Lexington. He was a ticket broker from Dallas, and he and his brother had just arrived in town for the game. I realized I'd been going to major sporting events for so long, I was starting to recognize the regulars!

After freshening at the hotel I dressed for the pursuit. The Celtics bring out the real basketball fans. That, combined with Houston being the hometown team, meant this would be a tough ticket. The pressure mounts!

Wearing coat and tie to look presentable in the eyes of would-be seat companions, I began the search outside the Summit. A young couple had an extra seat, but it was in the rafters. Not many tickets were available, and the few I found were way over-priced. I waited. About ten minutes before game time, two gentlemen offered an extra seat on the floor, no section number, for $100. This was a real find: in the premium seats reserved for season ticket holders only — the true Houston honchos. The section number on the ticket was blank. VIP, Row 2, Seat 33. On the playing floor level!

With the twin towers of Kareem Oladjuwan and Ralph Sampson, Houston fought off Robert Parrish, Kevin McHale, and B.J. Johnson to send the series back to Boston Garden. And there among the Houston honchos in the VIP seating was a very content Tennessee traveler seeing basketball like he'd never seen it before. I tried to recall the last time I attended a sporting event where an attractive waitress came by my seat to take a food and beverage order. Couldn't think of one. It seemed only fitting to cap this short, but action-packed journey with a frosty cold Lone Star.

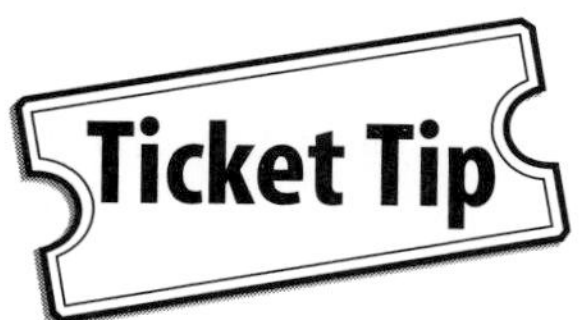

Look sharp when you're ticket shopping. Wear a jacket and tie. People are sizing you up not only as a buyer, but often as a prospective seating companion too. Honchos don't want to spend the afternoon sitting by some bum.

The Celtics won the next game in Boston, and eventually their sixteenth NBA title, interrupting the decade of dominance of Pat Riley's Los Angeles Lakers. Houston would not return to the NBA Finals until 1994, when they atoned for their defeat in '86 by winning the first of two back-to-back NBA championships.

An overnight whirlwind trip like this can be a little jewel of an adventure. It's all a matter of attitude and confidence. You can conjure up plenty of reasons to avoid acting on such a wild hair. The sensible choice is the mark of the masses; they miss the fun and the excitement!

Super Bowl — 1988

The Redskins' revenge

In January 1965, the Washington Redskins had just concluded another dreadful season. The 'Skins were known for always finding a way to lose, especially the close ones.

Earlier that season Richard Patterson, a hometown buddy who was in D.C. working for the FBI, sat with me in a steady downpour to watch Jim Brown churn the soggy turf at RFK Stadium as the Cleveland Browns bowled over the unfortunate 'Skins. Depressing as it was, I decided if I was going to live in Washington, I had a responsibility to root for the home team. Thus began my long love affair with the Redskins. My walk into the 'Skins small ticket office at 9th and H Streets that winter day set the stage for many memorable games. I wasn't much of a professional football fan at the time. Yet I bought four season tickets for the upcoming 1965 season, Section 526, Row 5, Seats 12-15. I still keep those seats warm a few Sundays every year.

Watching number nine, Sonny Jurgenson, sling the football for thirty-five yards across the field to Charley Taylor for a six-yard

gain was different from the college football I knew after twenty years as a spectator. Reading of the 'Skins tapping a place-kicker first in the draft was something you started to expect. (The logic of this pick would become apparent in the 1966 game with the New York Giants. The 'Skins were leading by a score of 69-41, when Otto Graham sent Charlie Gogalak in to attempt a field goal. His successful kick led to the final score of 72-41, the highest-scoring game in the history of the NFL. The record remains today!)

The one-year stint with Coach Vince Lombardi at the Redskins' helm was cut short after his 1969 season. A real loss to 'Skins fans and to everyone who loved football. We had envisioned Lombardi leading the 'Skins to the Super Bowl, becoming the first coach to lead two different teams to that championship. Gradually moving from the back of the pack, Washington made it to their first Super Bowl in 1973, only to face the Miami Dolphins, the first and only team to reach the Super Bowl undefeated. After the Super Bowl they remained undefeated.

Even though the game was played in the Rose Bowl, which seats over 100,000, Redskins season ticket holders never had a chance to buy tickets. The 'Skins' next Super Bowl trip had a lottery for season ticket holders, but I wasn't picked in 1983, nor for Super Bowl XVIII in 1984.

By the 1980s, Coach Gibbs had his team in the hunt for the championship every year, and I faithfully ordered NFC play-off tickets each time. When those games were played in Washington, tickets were available to the season ticket holders. During the 1987 season, as soon as it became apparent that the 'Skins might be Super Bowl-bound, I entered the drawing to apply for seats in San Diego comparable to my season tickets. This time my number came up — I would see the 'Skins in the Super Bowl. Over twenty years of patience finally was about to pay off.

Between the NFL championship and the Super Bowl, there was a lot to do. In less than two weeks I had to get my tickets, make travel arrangements, and be in San Diego. I didn't have time for tickets to reach me in Nashville from Washington, D.C., before I had to leave for the game. Carrol Carter, a friend in Washington, picked up my tickets and forwarded them overnight. Fans outside the ticket office tried to buy them from her as soon as she picked them up. Flights to San Diego had been filled long ago, so I flew into Los Angeles, picked up a car and stayed at North Island Naval Air Station, not far from NFL hotel headquarters at the Del Cornado Hotel.

Part of the fun in any major sporting is soaking in the total ambiance. You don't have to be registered at the team hotels or event headquarters to enjoy all the happenings. Sitting in the hotel lobby watching the players, coaches, and media celebrities come and go is something you'll never see on television. Combine these pre-game possibilities with side trips to local tourist attractions and you have the ingredients for a fantastic excursion.

Like so many Super Bowls, this one wasn't even close, but we Redskins enjoyed the 42-10 blowout. The special interest in this game was the incredible performance of a rookie running back for the Redskins, Timmy Smith. He gained over 200 yards rushing to set a Super Bowl record, but he has not been heard from since.

Doug Williams finally savored the taste of winning the big one, and John Elway, the Denver quarterback, had the elusive Super Bowl ring slip away for the second time. Since then, the Broncos have tied the dubious distinction set by the Minnesota Vikings and the Buffalo Bills of four Super Bowl trips and four second-place finishes.

What a change from the '60s. The Redskins were the doormat of the NFL then, and you could walk in off the street and buy four season tickets. As the '80s ended, Coach Gibbs had taken the 'Skins to the Super Bowl three times, with two championship rings to show for his trouble. Now the waiting list for season tickets is approaching 49,000. Jack Kent Cooke will fix that with his enviable new stadium in Raljon, Maryland, less than five miles from RFK.

Hail to the Redskins!

Bowled Over in '87

Aloha Bowl

What's another 5,000 miles?

I had plans to go to the Rose Bowl on New Year's Day, 1987. And since I was going to be heading west, I started looking around for other bowl games in the vicinity. There was the Freedom Bowl, and also the Holiday Bowl. My wife and I would be flying from Nashville to Salt Lake City to visit with our daughter over the holidays, and then continue on to Los Angeles. Well, somewhere in all of this planning I said, "Why don't we just go on to Hawaii?"

Of course, the Aloha Bowl is in Hawaii. And I had been challenged by my friend Fletch Lowe, who had seen two games in one bowl season. I had to beat his record.

Christmas Day found us

high over the Pacific enroute to Honolulu for the December 27 Aloha Bowl between the University of North Carolina and the University of Arizona. We'd come a long way, had a short amount of time, and no tickets. But tickets were a cinch. The locals didn't really turn out, and tourists were there for the beach, not the ball game. After buying tickets at the gate, I found that we could sit anywhere we wanted. One bowl game down, Rose Bowl tickets in hand, and beautiful Oahu all around.

We were to return to Los Angeles late on December 29. My wife reminded me that it was a midnight flight, which called for us to have an anniversary dinner complete with a picturesque Pacific sunset prior to departing the island. Combining sporting junkets with a special occasion is a great way to create a memorable experience for your spouse.

Freedom Bowl

The Green machine

Back in California after the Aloha Bowl, I saw that the Freedom Bowl would be played in Anaheim on December 30, with hometown favorite UCLA against Brigham Young. When Ginger and I got to Anaheim Stadium, we discovered that, like the Aloha Bowl, the Freedom Bowl didn't draw a large crowd. Again, we could sit anywhere we wanted to.

My greatest memory of that game was the UCLA running back Gaston Green. He had rushed for 1,139 yards and scored fourteen touchdowns for the 8-and-3 Bruins that year. And he led his Bruins to glory again that night.

However, an even larger human interest story emerged from the Cougar camp that year. BYU Coach Lavell Edwards was on his way to becoming a legend in Utah and in college football. Prior to his arrival, Brigham Young had won 171 games in forty-seven seasons. In his stint from 1972 to 1986, Coach Edwards won 137 games, eleven WAC titles (including ten in a row) and ten bowl games. In 1984 BYU won its National Championship.

Rose Bowl — 1987

Band in L. A.

Auburn coach Terry Bowden covered the 1995 Rose Bowl for NBC. He later commented about this game: “It’s someplace to go after the Rose Bowl Parade.” That attitude on the part of some fans was my ticket to the Rose Bowl in 1987.

Since people know of my love of sporting events, they enjoy challenging me with tales of their own exploits. Earlier, Fletch Lowe had been to two bowl games, and had thrown down the gauntlet at the 1986 Sugar Bowl. After this bowl season, I’d have an answer for him. I planned to build a trip around the Rose Bowl at year’s end. I’d never been to that bowl before, and through an unusual turn of events, this quest turned into one of my best ticket adventures ever.

Sometime during the year, I read in the local media that the Overton High School Band had been invited to march in the Rose Bowl Parade. So I started asking around to see if anybody knew anybody connected with the band. As luck would have it, a lady at work, Mrs. Gladys Wolfe, suggested I call Gary Dowdy, who had a son or daughter at Overton.

Gary was an eager and friendly source of information. Rose Bowl Parade Committee officials had visited Nashville in early December 1986 to give Overton the nod. They also had a drawing among the parents for who would go along as chaperones. An all-expense paid trip for Rose Bowl Parade week was the prize, including two seats to the Rose Bowl! I found out from Gary the name of the person who had won the drawing, and gave them a call. "Would you be interested in selling your game tickets?" I asked. "You bet! We'd rather have the money to shop," said the lady on the line, to my delight. They wanted more than face value for the tickets, but not an exorbitant amount, and we quickly made a deal.

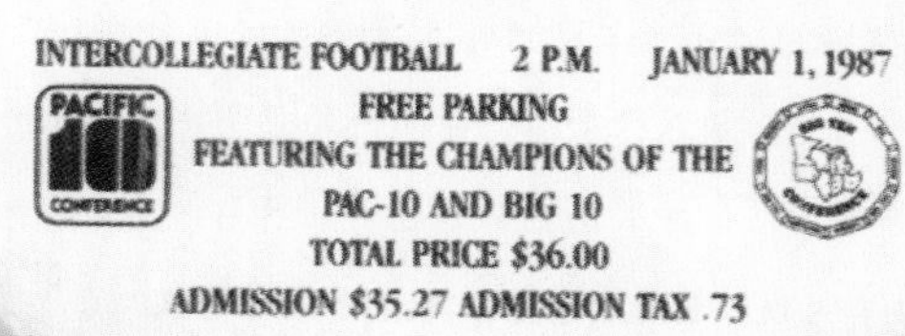

On a Sunday afternoon in December, we met to make the purchase. The chaperone was making the trip with a lady friend who

Great tickets can come from unlikely sources. Don't be afraid to ask.

was eager to watch their kids in the parade, but not eager to sit with 100,000 screaming people and watch a football game. I immediately checked the tickets against a Rose Bowl seating diagram, and saw that they were on the west side, the shady side, near the fifty-yard line, ten or so rows down in front of the press box, and on the aisle, seats 1 and 2. Just superb seats! Celebrity seats. Couldn't be better.

With tickets in hand I started working on enlarging the trip. I mentioned to my friend Buzz Davis that I was going to the Rose Bowl. He had a friend in the furniture business in Pasadena, Jack Biggars, who just happened to be the treasurer of the Tournament of Roses Committee that year. His furniture store was on Colorado Avenue, which was the main street for the parade.

Buzz kindly called Mr. Biggars about getting me a couple of Rose Bowl Parade tickets. Hundreds of thousands attend the Parade, spread over miles of bleachers and reserved seats. NBC, CBS, Fox, Tribune Broadcasting, Canadian Broadcasting Corporation, the Mexican network, and the Armed Forces Network would all cover the Parade, and all need room for commentators, celebrities, VIP guests, and so forth. The news from Mr. Biggars was that all of the reserved seats had been sold, but he would "check on it."

When I arrived in California on December 30, I went by his office to check on parade tickets. Too good to be true. The committee had had such a demand for seats that they had built another set of bleachers smack on the corner of Orange Grove and Colorado Avenue, the primary turning point of the Parade. And that's where I was. The broadcast booths for the networks were just across the street.

One was on Orange Grove, and the other was on the same side of the street around the turn, going down Colorado. Now I had Rose Bowl Parade tickets and a Rose Bowl game ticket — both in prime locations.

We'd been advised to come early to get parked and find our seats. The 98th Rose Bowl Parade would begin at 8:20 a.m., so we arrived in the 7 a.m. range and found a parking place, noting the thousands of people without seats who had camped out overnight along the parade route, lining miles of streets and sidewalks. We worked our way to our little corner of the world to watch what must be the greatest and most famous parade in the world. I have seen the Macy's Thanksgiving Day, and while it's certainly spectacular, it pales in comparison to the flowers and the floats that the Tournament of Roses entrants work on for a year.

Refer to stadium seating diagrams.They're a reliable way to judge the quality and value of a ticket.

The network commentators spent about three hours attempting to describe the beauty of these floats and the excitement racing through the air that crisp January morning. I won't attempt to rival them. Suffice it to say that it was a spectacularly unforgettable event. I have recommended it to some folks (including the Charlie Evers family, of Sunbeam Bakery in Nashville. I think my Rose Bowl account inspired him to go to the 100th Parade two years later.)

After the parade was over, we ambled down Rosemont Street to the "afterthought" to the Parade, the Rose Bowl Game. It was a gorgeous day in Pasadena. As I saw the stadium sprawling there at the foot of the hills, I reflected on my first memories of the Rose

Bowl. I could hear Bill Stern broadcast those ball games in the late '40s, when Michigan dominated the Pac-10 Conference in 1949, killing them with scores like 49-0. How times change. That bright New Year's Day, Arizona State handed Bo Schembechler's University of Michigan Wolverines a 22-15 defeat before 103,280 fans.

I had never seen the University of Michigan play, and I always liked their fight song, *Hail to the Victors.* I guess it is my favorite. I listened to the Blue and Maize band play it many times that day, valiant even in their losing cause. Sitting there in Section 19 Row 54 above the Rose Bowl Committee, the Tournament of Roses Committee, and the Rose Bowl Parade Queen, the day was another dream come true!

Fiesta Bowl

No-name national champs

After getting the Aloha Bowl and the Freedom Bowl under my belt, I was looking forward to the Rose Bowl on January 1. But wait. The Fiesta Bowl, the national college championship in Phoenix, had been moved from New Year's Day to January 2 in hopes of getting better media coverage. It pitted the Penn State Nittany Lions against the Miami Hurricanes for all the marbles.

After the Rose Bowl on January 1, the wheels begin to turn. "What would you say to a little jaunt to Phoenix?" I asked my patient wife. "I would say it doesn't surprise me in the least," she replied, eyes twinkling. So off we went. The first hurdle was a couple of plane tickets. Not many airlines were operating between Los Angeles and Phoenix.

Friday morning, January 2, 1987, we were at Los Angles International with bags in hand, ready to board a 7 a.m. flight for Phoenix. Fortunately the Fiesta Bowl was a night game. We had gotten plane tickets from a machine, the first I'd ever used. Insert your credit card, enter the data, and out they came. Vend-a-Flight. What will they think of next? I had called ahead to Avis in Phoenix for a car, but I decided to wait until I arrived to get a room. And, of course, we had no tickets.

After arrival, we headed immediately for the Arizona State campus to scope out the ticket market. Seeing some available, I relaxed a little, and Ginger and I left for a driving tour of Phoenix, a city new to her that I had visited several times. A motel room turned out to be a bit of a challenge. I wanted to get something near the airport, as I had already checked the flights out of Phoenix the next morning and knew we had to get an early start. We found a room near the airport all right. Noisy, tacky, and dirty. But close. Oh well, you can't win 'em all.

CONC STADIUM SUR & TAX INCL. WEST CONC

Catch a rising star!

Sunkist
Fiesta Bowl
XVI
January 1, 11:30 a.m.
Sun Devil Stadium
Tempe, Arizona

$25.00
SECTION
206
ROW
14
SEAT
1

Tickets for the game were expensive. After all, it was the National Championship. Fifty-yard-line seats low in the upper deck ran $125 each. Further shopping for a better price uncovered nothing. I paid the price, but the seats were worth it — fifty-yard line, lower portion of the upper deck, watching the battle for college football's number one ranking!

I'm a Joe Paterno fan, so I was pulling for Penn State. Ever since he declined the huge money offers from the New England Patriots, Coach Paterno has been one of my heroes. He announced that he would invest his time in developing young men, rather than pursue megabucks at the professional football level. This night the "no-name" jerseys of the Nittany Lions prevailed over Miami, 14-10. An interception by a linebacker, Shane Conlan who went on to play in the NFL, ended any hopes of a Miami win. Joe, you done us proud.

The next day, a seat on an eastbound Delta flight was out of the question. The Penn State and Miami fans were leaving Phoenix early. Northbound to Salt Lake City was a better prospect, but still dim. I told Ginger that we needed to be at the airport for the first launch and, after a short night in the Fleabag Arms, we got up before daylight to standby for the first Delta flight out of Phoenix to Salt Lake City. No room on that one. As luck would have it, two seats were available on the next flight an hour and a half later.

Soon we were back in Salt Lake City, where this incredible four-bowl odyssey began. Wonderful memories accompanied us — memories of beaches, roses, pineapple fields, desert beauty, an anniversary dinner overlooking the Pacific, western sunsets, and college football's finest. And those memories are with us still.

Grandstanding the Grand Slam

The Masters — 1993

The Best of Times

Most of the world's greatest sporting events are available to anyone with enough patience, cunning, and tenacity to get a ticket. You don't have to have megabucks; you don't have to know somebody with pull. You just have to keep your eyes and ears open, and be ready to act fast.

The Masters is an exception. I must admit that without the good fortune of having a close friend who's a member at Augusta National, I wouldn't stand a chance of waltzing through those gates to the immaculately manicured fairways. The tickets aren't that expensive, and the course is roomy and accommodating. It's just that the Masters was created by golfers, for golfers, to be an elegant statement of all the traditions that make golf what it is. They want the patrons to enjoy the tournament without crowding or in-

convenience. That means the number of admission badges is limited. Fans wait a generation for a badge, and when they finally get one, they have no intention of giving it up.

On a Thursday morning in early April, I boarded Shoney's MU-2 in Nashville, bound for Augusta at the invitation of Mr. Mike Rose. We were soon turning into the gates of Augusta National for the drive down Magnolia Lane. I had no way of knowing it at the time, but this drive would be the first leg of the Grand Slam of golf for me this year — the Masters, the U.S. Open, the British Open, and the PGA.

My host once again was Buzz Davis, who along with his wife, Florence, was staying in one of the cottages at the course. Buzz had rented the third and fourth floors of a huge antebellum house in Augusta for his guests. Other Masters fans occupied the first two floors. Each floor was a home within itself, complete with huge rooms, fourteen-foot ceilings, four bedrooms and baths, and a back porch for relaxing at day's end and recapping the shots and golfers we had seen.

At the Masters I usually begin the first day by walking the entire course. In the '60s I would follow my hero, Ben Hogan, for eighteen holes. Today I have no idol on the tour, so I will pick someone and follow them for a while until I lose interest. If someone is having a particularly great round, as Nick Price did in 1986 when he beat Lloyd Mangrum's 1940 record of 64 by one stroke, I'll fall in behind them. You can do this on Thursday or Friday without too much difficulty, unless your player is a crowd favorite like Jack Nicklaus. He will always have a huge following at Augusta.

Bernhard Langer won his second green jacket that year. I remembered seeing him in 1985 when he won his first one, a 27-year-old dressed in red from head to toe, with no U.S. victories on the tour and no indication he would soon move to the top of the leader board in golf's most prestigious competition.

In 1993 Langer was a different person — confident, successful, and a born-again Christian. God was first in his life by now, but golf and his family were close behind. He stepped up to the last hole, dressed tastefully in yellow and green, with a five-shot lead. His second green jacket complemented this ensemble a lot better than the first. He practically glowed with humble pride from within; pomp and adoration were obviously secondary. This winner in life is a worthy model for us all.

A ticket to the Masters is the most difficult ticket in sports. All the badges are sold to virtually the same list of patrons each year. The waiting list is closed, and reselling the badges is prohibited by the Augusta National Golf Club. Violators have their purchase privileges revoked and their name removed from the renewal list. So anyone who sells their tickets runs the risk of losing out for all future Masters tournaments. This penalty is severe, but enforced. Such prospects explain the prohibitive price of a ticket in the secondary market. At the 1995 SEC basketball tournament in Atlanta, one of the notable ticket hawkers said that he could get Masters four-day admissions for $3,500 per badge; practice round tickets would be $300 each. Yeow!

Counterfeiting these premium items is virtually impossible. Technology has allowed for numbers, holograms, and other secret doo-dads to be embedded in the badges for scanning at the admissions entrances. This has resulted in the most sophisticated ticket I am aware of.

One hint you might find useful: The last hope of legitimate entry without a Patron's badge is through the lotteries conducted for admission to the practice rounds.

A day walking the golf course with God's beautiful world all around is as good for rekindling the spirit as it is for watching the best players in the game.

U.S. Open — 1993

A hot time in the old town

Dr. Richard Terry, a fellow Tennessee Air National Guard member, had a smile on his face. We were at the Golf Club Of Tennessee on a Saturday in May, and he had just laid out the largest batch of golf tickets I had ever seen for the upcoming U.S. Open at Baltusrol: four sets of tickets to three practice rounds, four rounds of tournament play, and in the event of a tie, tickets for an eighteen-hole play-off on Monday. And on top of it all, he had tickets to park at Newark Airport for an air-conditioned bus ride through the New Jersey countryside.

Flying on American Airlines on the same flight were two other Nashville buddies, Marshall Polk and Alan Gore. As with many great sporting events, the U.S. Open had become an annual pilgrimage for these two gentlemen. For me it was a first. For golf it was the 93rd, the 88th under the PGA auspices. For Baltusrol, it was their seventh time to host the event, an Open record.

After a short trip from Newark Airport, the bus driver dropped us at the main entrance to Baltusrol Country Club. I decided to make my souvenir purchases early to avoid the weekend rush and picked-over merchandise. A huge vendors' tent was immediately inside the main entrance. Gathering up a slew of U.S. Open logo balls and an embroidered tapestry-type hang-up bag, my shopping was complete. No more golf shirts, sweaters, head covers, caps, and all that jazz, thank you. I've probably got a lifetime supply.

As I always do at Augusta, I immediately walked this

course, a new one for me. The old Baltusrol clubhouse, lodgings in an adjacent building, and the huge old trees lining the fairways offered testimony to the great traditions of this course. The club was organized in 1895 by Mr. Louis Kellar, a deaf farmer. He invited a group from the New York Social Register to join him for an annual fee of $100. Only nine holes were completed initially, with the second nine being added in 1896. After World War I, the members bought the land and retained Mr. Arthur Tillinghast to design and build two courses.

Our first day out was a scorcher — approaching 100 degrees. After six hours of watching golf in the heat and humidity we were more than ready for the air-conditioned ride to retrieve our car. Friday was more of the same. It was too hot to sit in that sun for any length of time. We found a grandstand on the back nine that was in the shade, but it just was not very exciting.

With the Masters being played at Augusta National every year, you become familiar with each hole and can anticipate some of the action. Not so with events that change venues every year, like the U.S. Open. We didn't know where to expect the most interesting play, but the par-five 17th hole gave us a bit of a show. John Daly was the first ever to reach this 630-yard hole in two shots. The 18th hole was different from some championship courses, in that it was viewed as the easiest hole on the course, another par five at 542 yards with a challenging tee shot. Some players use an iron to avoid the creek that cuts across the sloping fairway. A well-placed drive could leave a reachable second shot up the hill to a well-protected green. The past three times the U.S. Open was held at Baltusrol, 72-hole tournament records were tied or broken.

Lee Janzen was the eventual winner that year, tying the Open record of 272. Jack Nicklaus had broken the Open record originally in 1967 at Baltusrol, only to return in 1980 and set a new 72-hole record of 272. For all the firsts unveiled on that storied course, Dr. Terry, our friend Tom Herbert, and I never made it to the final round. To our mutual surprise, the three of us were thinking alike. Saturday night at dinner we tiptoed around the subject of leaving early. All three of us had had enough of the heat, the turnpikes, and the Newark environs. After an early Sunday flight to Nashville, the final round with the New York throngs would go on without these Southern boys.

By noon that Sunday, Dr. Terry and I were back at the Golf Club of Tennessee clubhouse where this adventure began. Only a few days ago our trip to the U.S. Open had been nothing but dreams and a lot of hot air. Now it was a shared experience, the beginning of another sporting memory to last a lifetime. We had returned to the familiar setting of a spaciously uncrowded golf course in Kingston Springs, Tennessee, ready to put our new shot-making skills to the test. We donned our spikes and walked through the quiet to the first tee. A long way from Newark, thank goodness.

The British Open — 1993

The Fleeing Scotsman

After returning from the U.S. Open, I trained my sights on what the Scots and English refer to as "The Open," or what we

colonists insist on calling the British Open. After securing an overseas flight on Delta, I called my principal in a venture called Golf in Scotland. Mr. Sam Harris arranges hotels, tee times, and a courier to escort visiting golfers at any of the 522 courses in Scotland. The news was good. "I have a few groups attending The Open this year at Royal St. Georges," he reported, "primarily French groups. It would be no problem to meet you there."

Course tickets would be no problem either, according to Sam, and he would check on accommodations around Royal St. Georges in the town of Sandwich, about sixty miles east of London. (It's also the name of the eighteenth century earl who, in order to gamble through lunch, had his servant bring meat between two pieces of bread to him at the card table.) I told Sam I planned to arrive next Wednesday, the day before the first round. To my astonishment, Sam drove down from Scotland to Gatwick Airport in London, some 425 miles, to meet me.

After a shower and change in Gatwick's Forte Hotel, we were on our way to Sandwich in the county of Kent. Sam drove us through Canterbury and on to the North Sea coast. I assumed Sam knew the way to our accommodations, and I was already imagining a picturesque country inn and a piping hot dinner awaiting our arrival. It was only after driving through three or four little seaside towns that Sam finally admitted we did not have a place to stay. The plot thickens.

As we went through one of the round-abouts approaching Sandwich from the north, I noticed a subtle rectangular sign pointing to RAF Manston. Royal Air Force. Wonder if they could put up an American reserve officer and his friend, should the need arise? We continued on south to Dover, where several imposing hotels perched on the hillside leading down to the famous white cliffs and the ferry landings. I had no idea the town had so many accommodations. Sam looked around a bit, checked for rooms at maybe two places, then drove us back north to Sandwich. He stopped at the office that every little British town has for booking a local hotel or bed and breakfast. Of course, the place was booked solid because of The Open.

There was nothing else to do but head to a pub for bitters and late lunch. Afterwards, I suggested that we go back to the Royal Air Force installation at Manston, where I had seen the sign earlier, to see if they could help us. He reluctantly agreed. At the time, I had no idea how reluctantly.

Security at military installations in Europe is tighter than we're used to in the U.S. As we approached the gate, the guards stood at attention for our arrival and my question. After presenting my U.S. military identification card, the security police allowed me to telephone the Officers' Billeting office to speak with the club manager. I explained our predicament, and asked if he could accommodate me and a Scottish national who was traveling with me. I figured we could spend the night, get my jet lag behind me, then find something in a nearby town the next day.

The manager was very obliging. "I do have some rooms," Adrian reported shortly, "and you are both most welcome." Sam instructed me to go register, and suggested I rest and recharge my battery from my overnight flight. In the meantime he would scout the countryside for a clean, reasonably priced room or bed and breakfast for us for the balance of the week. Sounded like a good plan.

After a nap, I dressed for dinner at the club, and shared a table with some hospitable young RAF radar control trainees. Later I retired to the reading room where coffee, cigars, and newspapers constituted the evening's entertainment. I had been nestled in one of those big stuffed leather chairs for a while when the bartender glided up and said, "Brigadier, you have a message at the main gate." My rank was no secret among the very proper yet polite English employees.

I wasn't expecting a message, but this one was a doozy. Sam, the Scotsman, had written that he could not stay on an *English* base and was returning to Glasgow! His earlier description of the locals in Newcastle as "Scots who've had their heads bashed in" now took on a clearer meaning. (He did leave me some new brochures and a videotape of the Scottish Open Golf Courses for promoting our Golf in Scotland tours, though I could hardly recommend them at that moment.)

Here I was on an RAF base in eastern England, without a car, without Open tickets . . . stranded. At this late hour, considering my combination of jet lag, surprise, and irritation, I decided to take Scarlett's advice in *Gone With The Wind:* "I'll worry about it tomorrow."

As I had hoped, my attitude was much improved after a good night's sleep. No ticket? No ground transportation? No problem! Little details like that weren't going to keep me from enjoying the British Open I'd come three thousand miles to see. In the world of sports tickets, one of the keys to success is a positive attitude.

I learned that a commercial air terminal was located on the other side of the base. That was going to be my best bet for ground transportation to the Royal St. George Golf Course, some three or four miles away. I walked to the commercial terminal in a light drizzle, across the public thoroughfare that crosses the runways. (This is a fairly common practice in the British Isles.) As luck would have it, a bus was operating every couple of hours to The Open, returning in the late afternoon. Transportation problem solved!

Tickets were plentiful at the gate, with £20 the price of a full day's activities. Only hours after being abandoned by my Fleeing Scotsman, I had tickets, room, and transportation taken care of.

My biggest awakening with the British Open was the commercialization of the event. I expected that an event sponsored by the Royal and Ancient Golf Association would be as strict and tradition-oriented as the golf rules at St. Andrews. The British Open, one of the oldest trophies in sports, goes back to an inaugural match at Old Prestwick, Ayr, Scotland, in 1860. Today, huge corporate tents were everywhere, far more spectacular than what I had seen at the U.S. Open in Baltusrol.

Sam liked to tell a story that illustrates how strict the rules are at St. Andrews. A Malaysian king was to play the Old Course and was late for his tee time. When he finally arrived, ready and anxious to get going, His Majesty was informed that "the starter of St. Andrews does not even wait for a king."

As usual, I did my shopping ahead of time, with raingear against the drizzle as my first purchase. One of my weaknesses is golf memorabilia, especially old putters. I had to buy a wooden putter made in St. Andrews. In part I was replacing a similar putter I had bought at

Harrod's in London several years before, but had given to Buzz. I knew he loved old putters too, and loved putting enough to have a putting green in his back yard in Nashville. (He continues to experiment with the latest putter technologies — hoping to improve his stroke, I presume.)

In addition to the rain jacket, I found logo balls, ball marks, head covers, and Open score cards to complete the minimum mandatory souvenir buy. After all, the 122nd occurrence of anything is worth a few overpriced and non-essential treasures.

As usual I walked the course, beginning at number one and hop-scotching around the eighteen holes. At each hole was a Rolex tee marker with the hole number, distance, and the line, "We make every round in 60 seconds." And the correct time, of course.

British Open venues seem to have more seating capacity than those in the U.S. This tournament had 15,000 grandstand seats, with almost thirty rows of bleachers on the 18th green. It's like hitting into an open-air arena as the golfers converge onto the green at the end of the 18th fairway.

My first day concluded back at the RAF Officers' Club with an enjoyable encounter just before dinner. I had changed into the recommended coat and tie and had walked to the terrace with my draft beer to enjoy the waning sunset. The day had cleared, and it was a beautiful July evening. I was reflecting on the day's events and such a fitting end to a marvelous day, when the bartender called out, "Brigadier, the Air Commodore would like for you to join him for a drink."

My mind was racing. "An Air Commodore is my peer, I think." The RAF rank structure had its beginnings in Britain's historic naval power, with navy ranks being adapted for use in the Royal Air Force.

Keeping a positive attitude will improve your chances of success. The more you're convinced that you'll get the ticket you want, the more likely it is you'll get it.

A one-star naval officer was a Commodore. Thus, an RAF one-star general officer became known as an Air Commodore. My muddling recollection of comparable ranks was interrupted by a friendly introduction. The distinguished-looking gentlemen who had offered me a drink was retired from the military and now an executive with British Aerospace, working for his former RAF commander in the company's military division. He and his ex-commander, along with their wives, were staying at the Club and attending The Open, just as I was.

When his boss, the former Air Chief Marshal of the RAF, arrived, his warmth immediately put me at ease. Two avid golfers who also were retired Air Force officers had to be great guys. The proper title for the Air Chief Marshal's wife was beyond my alarmingly poor recollection of protocol. An evening with British aristocracy probably exposed many social woes of this slow-talking Tennessean. In spite of that they were very gracious.

After they left for a seafood dinner in Sandwich, I think I got it all sorted out. The Air Commodore and his wife, John and Wendy Mitchell, were a delight, and we have continued to correspond with the hope of seeing each other again. The Air Marshal and his wife, Sir Patrick and Lady Hines, overlooked my social faux pas with the easy grace that is the mark of true aristocrats.

Friday I once again marched to the commercial terminal for the short trip to Royal St. George. No word came from Sam in Glasgow. I was not very happy with Mr. Sam Harris, and I did not intend to telephone him. At The Open the Americans were back in the pack. I followed Fred Couples, Lee Janzen, and Jack Nicklaus, pulling my hardest for the red, white, and blue. Greg Norman was playing very well.

On this beautifully sunny and breezy day, I was standing on a knoll along the right side of the #10 fairway, at the landing area for the tee shots. I could look across holes 11 and 12, out to the North Sea. Two Englishmen were talking while we waited for the next group to hit their second shots on this slightly uphill 401-yard par four. As we watched a ferry in the distance headed for France, one man asked the other, "Do you know how many crossings there are every day across the Straits of Dover?" His friend had no idea. "Three hundred." To that, his companion replied, "Are you sure about that?" The first man answered proudly, "I don't give away useless information that's inaccurate!" Only in England.

While following the golfers was fun, I had to begin to ponder my return trip. No Sam Harris to help on the return to Gatwick. Probably better that way.

During the day, I checked on Delta for the return flights, and decided to try for Saturday, as the Sunday flights in the summer from Europe to the U.S. are heavily traveled. After bidding farewell to RAF Manston on Saturday morning, I checked my bags at Royal St. Georges, then took a look at the train schedule from Sandwich to London's Victoria Station. There I would change trains for Gatwick Airport.

(One of the special joys of traveling in England is sampling all the forms of transportation. After you arrive, probably by plane, you may find yourself on double-decker buses, trains, ferries, taxis, or one of the Chunnel trains under the English Channel. The Old Country has so much to sample.)

But before I left, I still had another beautiful day of the British Open ahead at the links course overlooking the North Sea. A room awaited me at the Forte House south of London adjacent to the Gatwick Airport. Everything was squared away with no unknowns for my return flight west, filled with fresh memories of one of sport's great weeks.

I decided to ride first class on the train to London and enjoy the late afternoon vistas in spacious luxury. Summer sunsets are late in those northern latitudes, so my trip through the countryside took us toward the last rays of light disappearing over the horizon. The spacious, quiet first-class car encouraged me to let my thoughts run over the last few days — Sam's unexpected disappearance, the hospitality of the RAF, and the good company of the Air Commodore and Lord and Lady Hines. What a shame it had to end.

I now had three legs of the Grand Slam in the same year. My thoughts turned to the PGA and the final gem in golf's greatest spectacle.

PGA —1993

A Daly inspiration

Compared to England, Ohio was practically in my back yard. And a trip to the PGA Tournament in Toledo was the only thing between me and the completion of a longtime dream — seeing all four tournaments in the Grand Slam of Golf in one year. With three weeks between the

You can often save on travel expenses by flying to a bigger city reasonably near your event, renting a car at the airport, then driving to the target destination.

British Open and the PGA, and this being the least famous of the four events, I had plenty of time to make arrangements.

Tickets at Inverness Golf Club were plentiful. I flew into Detroit from Nashville and rented a car, drove directly to the Inverness parking lot, and bought a one-day ticket. This course, as most of the northern-tier courses, has those rolling, tree-lined fairways ending in bent grass greens varying in size from huge to minuscule. Quite frankly, without a pal to share the day, this course did not hold the excitement as the three previous legs of the Grand Slam.

As with all of the rotating tournaments, the local golf association had been working a couple of years in advance to make their week in the golfing spotlight a complete triumph. The volunteer workers at these tournaments are the unsung heroes of the sport. Polite, helpful, and cheerful, they are ready with information on practically everything, and are always eager for out-of-town guests to leave with a favorable impression of their home city. At all these tasks, the Inverness people were a rousing success!

John Daly drew my attention for the day's play. I usually follow the more traditional golfers, where I may pick up a pointer, or learn from their reactions to failures and successes. (Ben Hogan was my first idol and remains my all-time favorite golfer. His style and manner shaped my own approach to golf.)

As a medium handicap golfer after forty years at the game, I found the way Daly lashed into a tee shot to be absolutely unbelievable. I suppose I was watching the longest hitter in the history of the PGA tour. On one par four — the #4 hole, I think — I stood behind the tee as John pulled out his one-iron. At the 310-yard position on the hole a steep hill fell away, making a very difficult downhill lie for the second shot. John unleashed his tee shot down the middle. As I walked to his second shot, John walked past me and much of the rest of the gallery. He is one of the fastest players on the tour, and he had hit his second shot by the time I got to where his tee shot had landed. One of the marshals told me Daly's shot was 300 yards.

After two enjoyable days on the course, I went home and watched the final two rounds on TV. Paul Azinger and Greg Norman eventually tied after 72 holes, and Azinger won a sudden-death play-off.

Two years later, John Daly was playing in The Vinny, a charity event for young golfers hosted by country music superstar Vince Gill at the Golf Club of Tennessee. I watched John hit a drive on the fifth hole, a par five that measured 533 yards from the back tees. The collective "Ahhh!" from the gallery was evidence we all thought we had just seen a monster shot. When we got to his ball, he was inside the 212-yard marker on a sprin-

kler head. His caddie told him he was 202 yards to the pin. He had hit the tee shot 331 yards to a perfect position!

On his second shot, with a six iron, he came off the shot a bit and hit right into the woods; the third went out of the woods across the green into the deep weeds. He hit his fourth shot onto the green and two-putted for a bogey. Daly's fans follow him for his airmail drives, not his final score.

(As I write this account, I've just watched John on TV playing the 18th hole in the third round of the 1995 British Open at St. Andrews. His tee shot rolls up the hill to the left of the green and rolls back. His second shot is six to eight feet past the pin. He sinks the putt for a birdie. The next day Daly wins the Claret Cup. His name is etched on the oldest trophy in golfing history!)

Unlike Sandwich or St. Andrews, Toledo is a large populated area that absorbs the PGA crowd with hardly a ripple. I am not so sure that the locals where I ate dinner even knew a tournament was going on, much less that it was the final leg of the Grand Slam of golf. They don't know what they're missing! I missed having a comrade to replay the day's adventure with. Once again I was reminded that, though traveling alone is better than staying home, any experience is richer when you have someone to share it with.

Sterling Cups

World Cup — 1986

Fútbol fever

Even though I had been introduced to soccer at the USAF Squadron Officers School in 1964, the sport never had captured my attention. At that time few in America were captured by the sport, even though it's a huge favorite on the International sports scene.

I got another taste of soccer in the spring of 1982, when a YMCA friend of mine asked if I would assist in coaching the youth soccer league. Since I had some very, very limited playing experience, the head coach, Jim Barr, thought I could help in coaching the fundamentals. These six-, seven-, and eight-year-old boys and girls captured my heart with their naiveté and enthusiasm. The natural athletes in the bunch required little instruction, and those who played more for the team experience needed only encouragement and reassurance. For three years, I got far more than I gave. Those youngsters were a pleasure to be around.

In late spring 1986, my modest interest in the world's most popular sport was stoked by newspaper coverage of the World Cup in Mexico City. When the Cup pairings were announced, I began feeling an urge to head south of the border. The preliminary matches were scattered throughout Mexico, and the logistics of getting to any of them made a trip to the hinterlands out of the question. But the semifinals and finals would be in the capital city.

My daughter was able to get a travel pass courtesy of her employer, Western Airlines. But the closest city to Nashville served by Western was St. Louis. As luck would have it, a cousin who built drag racing hulls had to drive to St. Louis for a race on the weekend of the soccer finals. There was my ride to St. Louis.

Cousin Sherman dropped me at a motel near the St. Louis airport on a Friday night for an early morning flight to Los Angeles. I got my first taste of soccer excitement in the Los Angeles airport, where the crowd gathering for the L.A./Mexico City flight was huge and causing chaos. Since I was traveling standby, my prospects looked grim. When the boarding call was announced, I began to count the number of passengers entering the passage way. More people had to be in the waiting area than the number of available seats. Finally all ticketed passengers were boarded, and the agent began to call up the standbys. A few couples and families opted not to split up. As "Newcomb" came over the speaker, I realized that I had the last seat on board! Center seat on the right side near the back of a jam-packed airplane. But I was on board.

After the three-and-a-half hour flight, I arrived in the most populated city in the world. Once I cleared customs, I called the Hilton to see if a room was out of the question. "I need it for two nights," I replied to the impeccable English-speaking hotel clerk. No problemo.

It was a rainy, dreary evening as the taxi driver took me to this Americanized oasis surrounded by the teeming city. After checking in, I went down to the restaurant, which had the feel of a United Nations conclave without the diplomats. The place was crazy with Germans unfurling their flag of horizontal red, black, and gold stripes. I've always had trouble telling their flag from Belgium's. Both were there, and both have the same colors, with one running horizontally and the other vertically. The English were there in strength as well, along with some other players whose teams had already been eliminated.

Sunday's premier match pitted England against Argentina and their world-famous star Diego Maradona. At the entrance to the hotel was a huge pairings board with the participants' national flags, showing all the remaining semifinalists. As I stood admiring the display, I noticed another chap beside me doing likewise. In my southern accent I asked him, hoping he spoke English, if he was going to Aztec Stadium for the game. He replied cordially with a proper British accent. I suggested we share a taxi, and he quickly agreed. After a ride filled with pleasant conversation about his traveling 5,500 miles for a couple of weeks of soccer, we separated for life.

The sun shone brightly in Mexico City's thin air, 7,300 feet above sea level. My immediate challenge was finding a ticket in the vast concrete area surrounding Aztec Stadium. I'd have to manage without some of the tools of the trade. I didn't have a seating chart. I didn't know what tickets were worth, either in pesos or dollars. I didn't know the language, which was an adventure in itself. But I relished the hunt and was determined to learn as I went.

Between getting quotes on tickets, I visited the pin collector booths and the individual huddles where collectors swapped merchandise. Gradually, by comparing the face value printed on the tickets, I gained a sense of the best seat locations. I didn't know if these tickets were like bullfight tickets in Madrid, where the shady seats command premium prices.

When you're looking for tickets outside the U.S., here are three things you should have:
1) an understanding of what the local currency is worth in dollars;
2) a seating chart of the sporting venue, or some idea of where the good and bad seats are;
3) some way of communicating — knowing a little of the local language is extremely helpful.

I eventually found a box seat that brought a whole new meaning to my definition of the term. I was literally enclosed in a box. No one else ever arrived to join me. Maradona put on his predictable performance as promised, leading Argentina to a win with a late score.

My early check-out the next morning gave me the chance to eavesdrop on an international financial transaction. A German guest was trying to check out with a credit card that was not recognized by the hotel. As best as I could tell, he had been there for three weeks, and had run up a bill of over three thousand U.S. dollars. The conversion to marks was going to require a phone call to his bank in Bonn. What puzzled me was why a German would stay in Mexico City three weeks, then leave before Germany played Argentina for the World Cup. Maybe he anticipated the eventual outcome. Maradona led Argentina to the Championship, their second in eight years.

Had I known the World Cup would be hosted by the U.S. in 1994, I might have waited until then and had a shorter trip. But on second thought, a jaunt to Washington, D.C., or Atlanta would never have matched the thrill of the unknown that marked the way to Mexico.

America's Cup — 1995

Gone again

The British Open dates back to 1860, the Kentucky Derby to 1875, the Belmont Stakes to 1867, and the Stanley Cup to 1893. But the oldest trophy in sports is the America's Cup, a bottomless silver Victorian pitcher named after the first ship to win it. An American crew brought it home to New York in 1851 after defeating their English counterparts in a race around the Isle of Wight off the southern coast of England. Thus the sailing world gave birth to one of the most infrequently yet hotly contested prizes in sports history.

Since the original contest there have been 29 challenges. The winner of the last competition sets the time and place of the next challenge. The erratic schedule adds to the allure. Originally, the

Spectator Cruise Ticket
America's Cup '95 № 02070
DATE: MAR 25 1995
RACE
DEFENDER/CHALLENGER SERIES (JAN- FEB)
SEMI - FINALS (MARCH)
FINALS (APRIL)
MATCH RACES (MAY)
SAN DIEGO HARBOR EXCURSION
1050 NORTH HARBOR DRIVE SAN DIEGO, CA 92101
(619) 234-4111 OR (800) 44-CRUISE (442 -7847)
(Non-refundable)
Race dates subject to change
ADMIT ONE GUEST
Valid for passage only on above date

challengers had to sail their sloops to the defending country's course. All of these nuances are a huge departure from the predictability offered by every other major sporting event.

Why do I even mention the America's Cup, when it appeals primarily to an elitist following and can barely be called a spectator sport? When the cost of entering a competitive team can reach $45 million and require years to ready a hull and bring a team together? Some may even ask, "Is it a sporting event at all?"

Where there is competition and the will to win, there's sport. Even if you have to watch it through binoculars.

Besides, it was another ticket to try for.

My first awareness of the America's Cup race was just before the 1980 challenge off the coast of Newport, Rhode Island. Some buddies at the Air National Guard returned from a conference at Quonset Point raving about the beautiful racing ships moored at Newport. Over the next few years, I became more aware of the growing popularity of sailing as I witnessed the motorless boats on Percy Priest Lake near the Nashville Airport. Some of the Air Guard guys bought them in a partnership. Easier to justify to skeptical family members, I suppose.

In 1983, America lost the cup for the first time ever. In February 1987, with the Cup in Australian hands, American television covered the races in Freemantle. The time differential with Australia made for some late-night viewing, but as I watched, the uniqueness of the sport intrigued me:

■ The crew members: a unique and specific task for each.

■ The use of technology: designing the most efficient use of the hull.

■ The uncontrollable wind: the strategy required to cope with Mother Nature's all-important variable.

■ The leadership skills: a true team captain, not just a figurehead.

■ A classic tournament format: every team facing every other team in the challenge meets.

■ The international aspect of the competition: the USA against the world.

I liked that package — weather, individual skills, teamwork, leadership, technology, and the tug of patriotism.

When the U.S. brought the Cup back home after beating the Aussies in 1987, I filed the America's Cup away as a worthy event to try for. Unlike the regularly scheduled Olympics or World Cup, it might be two, three, four, or five years before the next America's Cup race. Another variable is the race venue, selected by the defenders. The U.S. could choose either the Atlantic or Pacific Ocean. Dennis Conner, who had lost the Cup in '83 and regained it in '87, naturally chose his home course at the San Diego Yacht Club. In addition to Australia and other international challengers, he would have some home grown competition too, in the form of an all-female crew on the *Young America*, sponsored by Mr. Bill Koch. And, oh by the way, Koch would invest approximately $45 million in the enterprise.

There were two brackets to the competition. The Citizen Cup was for American crews who wanted to challenge Dennis Conner for the right to defend the title. The Louis Vuitton Challenge was a series of races among all the challenging nations to determine who would take on the Americans.

As a member of the Employers' Support for Guard and Reserve committee, I would be traveling to San Diego in March. This trip had been scheduled for more than six months, and when it was set I had no idea that the America's Cup would be underway off Point Loma.

When we arrived, all the international sailing teams were moored at Shelter Island. After the first evening in San Diego, a few us went down to the waterfront and stumbled upon Dennis Conner's entry, Stars and Stripes. The next day, during our bus tour of the military installations in and around San Diego, I asked our driver about the America's Cup. How do you see the races? He told us excursion boats went out to the courses each morning.

Tickets for the America's Cup races are available by the boatload. There's no other box office experience like it.

The hotel concierge booked me for a Saturday excursion. Our escort for the Guard trip arranged quarters for me at the Marine Amphibious Base on Coronado Island. I was set.

I got my shopping done early, with a rain jacket and cap, et cetera, from Dennis Conner's *Stars and Stripes* collection. Next I thought I'd have a look at those beautiful yachts. But trying to get near them was like trying to enter a nuclear submarine base. Security was tight, except the *Young America*'s team, which was allowed a freer access. On Saturday morning *Young America*'s invited guests, corporate sponsors, and others brunched, then boarded their excursion boat for the race with *Stars and Stripes.*

What a contrast: men versus women (except the helmsman, who joined the crew after the competition began); tradition versus the new kid on the block; the America's Cup Championship team versus the untested. After absorbing the morning excitement at the *Young America*'s dock, I drove to the marina to board my excursion boat.

"This is the way to see an event," I thought, lounging on the deck a few minutes later, surrounded by attentive food and drink service. We were moving through San Diego harbor toward the race course, past the aircraft carriers *USS Eisenhower* and *Kitty Hawk*. I had been on board the *Kitty Hawk* the previous day, and now enjoyed another perspective of that floating 1,000-foot landing strip.

Just past Point Loma, all the entries, officials, media, safety boats and others like us were arrayed on the water. My fellow passengers obviously knew far more of the jargon, rules, and tactics than I did. A couple from St. Paul, Minnesota, was tolerant enough to indulge a Nashvillian in his quest for sailing knowledge. They had been here in 1992, they said, and would be back for the finals in this competition. The young people aboard clung to the rail, freely offering their views as two sloops whipped extremely close to our boat. The racers had begun jockeying for position to enter the starting triangle five minutes prior to the scheduled start time.

No coin tosses, no starting blocks, no umpire calling, "Play ball," no line-ups based on qualifying times. It's only the skill of the crew and the five-minute horn before the scheduled start. The skippers directed the action, maneuvering sloops forty-four feet long at the water line with four sails of varying spans and a crew of nine working in unison. All were preparing to cope with an ally and enemy that they couldn't even see — the wind. It's like no other start I had ever seen, including "Gentlemen, start your engines."

"I must be mellowing," I thought, because the sheer joy of being on the ocean on a cloudless day in seventy-degree temperatures to watch a slow moving competition brought a welcome sense of relaxation. It was every bit as great as a heart-pounding Indianapolis start.

We tracked along outside the prescribed course of *Stars and Stripes* down to the turning point, some three miles away. We followed this race for a while and then moved to another course six or eight miles to the north to watch the New Zealand team, the eventual Cup winner, defeat the Japanese. A day on the water off the coast of San Diego makes you appreciate why the Californians cherish their beaches and water sports.

By the middle of May, the New Zealand team would sweep the U.S. 4-0, handing America its second loss in the history of the trophy. Unfortunately *Stars and Stripes* was the defeated vessel both times. There's no doubt in my mind that America's best is already at work to bring back that Cup, combining computer chip technology with man's age-old struggle against the wind. Their perseverance over months and years of preparation should be an inspiration to athletes everywhere.

Sporting competitions are usually tense situations, with boisterous fans packed into a stadium or arena filled with eighteen-inch seats. Not so with the America's Cup. The calm of the event is incredibly therapeutic and uplifting. It's probably the most serene setting for any sports competition I've ever witnessed.

Stanley Cup NHL Championship — 1995

Devilish delights

During the National Hockey League play-offs of '95, I started pulling for the teams closest to Nashville. The St. Louis Blues went early, but Chicago, Detroit, and Pittsburgh advanced. When Chicago and Detroit advanced to the semis, I could follow a team fairly close to Nashville. If there was an afternoon match-up in the Stanley Cup, I could possibly manage a one-day trip.

But I'm getting ahead of the story.

With Nashville constructing a new $120 million arena and in hot pursuit of the New Jersey Red Devils, hockey fever was sweeping the city. At least, the radio sports talk shows and the news media kept the prospects tantalizing. When the New Jersey team beat the Philadelphia Flyers to advance to the finals, the drumbeats grew louder. The pending move of Mr. Mc Mullen's hockey team created lots of controversy in both cities. Of course, Governor Whitman in New Jersey did not relish the prospect of losing this professional

RW4P: EVENT CODE SECTION 213B ROW 1 SEAT 14 $ W INCL. CITY SERV. FEE
$ 100 00 SECTION 213B $
INCL. CITY SERV. FEE
SECT 213
CA 1
ROW 1 SEAT
4121
W14J
STANLEY CUP FINALS
DETROIT RED WINGS
5x VS.....
14 HOME GAME "P"
12 JOE LOUIS ARENA
N5 DATE/TIME T.B.A.

franchise. When the team began advancing through the play-offs, she summoned Mr. Whitman for a little chat between the New Jersey Sports Authority and the Red Devil management.

The escalating estimate for the Nashville arena created some turmoil at first. Then people seemed to decide, "Well, that's what it takes to get a major league sports franchise." All that changed, however, when someone pointed out that the arena was going up within one-hundred feet of the First Baptist Church, which meant it couldn't sell beer. Big trouble. Special legislation was proposed. As a First Baptist Church member, I felt close to the debate. Eventually, legislation was passed to exempt the arena from the 100-foot rule.

With that background, and with a potential Stanley Cup Championship team coming to Nashville, my Stanley Cup planning began. With juice and coffee and the *USA Today* ticket section in front of me, I got down to work on the backyard patio. Yellow pages and a cordless phone were the only tools required.

Southwest had a flight to Detroit, arriving at 2:30 p.m. on game day and returning the next morning by 10:30 a.m. I had to buy it five days in advance. Automobile and hotel were easy, inexpensive, and both cancellable. Now came the tough one — the ticket. Detroit had played hockey for seventy years, winning seven Stanley Cup Championships, but had not contended for the Cup since 1966, and hadn't won since '55. The Detroit Cougars had joined the NHL in an expansion in 1926, changed their name to the Falcons in 1930, and had been known as the Red Wings since 1933. Their fans' twenty-nine-year hunger was about to be satisfied. They were in the finals at last.

I was looking for one seat in an arena that held 19,275, including standing room. Finding one would be easy. Finding a trustworthy seller and a good price were the obstacles. I had decided to pay a maximum of somewhere in the $250 range. Should I buy ahead of time, or wait until game night to try my luck outside the arena? I had always been lucky, but this may be the last of my top twenty-five major events. Twenty-four down and one to go! I did not want any unnecessary risks. (Wimbledon in 1996 changed this.)

I called several of the ticket brokers advertising in *USA Today*. It was the first time I had ever taken that route. On my first call, prices ranged from $250 to $900. Of course the $250 seat would be in the rafters and I didn't bother asking the location of the $900 seat. I had the Joe Louis Arena seating diagram in front of me. After those calls, I had a feel for the market. With the game still seven days away, I decided to wait.

On Thursday, I called my cousin Earl Brown at Pontiac Motors in Pontiac, Michigan. After a little research, he guessed I would have to pay $300 for rinkside within ten rows of the ice. I knew the ticket broker had to have a margin of profit, but I suspected that Earl was low on his estimate and the brokers were high on their asking price.

Earl checked with his brother-in-law, who was a general manager for a minor league hockey team in Detroit and others locally. Nothing. I was back to square one. I called Southwest Airlines and asked for a twenty-four-hour extension on my airfare commitment, which they kindly agreed to.

Next morning I was back on the phone to the ticket brokers. Some had no tickets left. One did not deal in singles. Two did not bother to return my call. I even offered one broker the opportunity to help him in the future: mention his firm in this book. Too bad I never heard back from Claudio.

At 9 p.m. Friday I confirmed my non-refundable reservation on Southwest. Now I was committed! I felt that if the Red Wings lost the first game at home, tickets might loosen slightly. A sweep of Detroit was highly unlikely, so they would return for game five and, if it went seven games the championship would be at Joe Louis Arena.

I decided to check the Detroit ticket brokers again on Monday after the Red Wings' Saturday loss. A trip to the Nashville library provided a copy of the *Detroit Times-Free Press* ticket section. There seemed to be ample tickets, but prices were firm and expensive. One broker hung up when I made a counter offer to his asking price.

Too much was at stake to risk being shut out for the first time in over forty-five years. This was for the last milestone in my life-long pursuit of what I considered to be the greatest sporting contests in the world. A Stanley Cup match at the home site of a team with a seventy-year history and seven titles, but no Cup in forty years.

For once I opted for the cautious, safe approach. I finally struck a deal with a broker for a single on the first row of the second level. The ticket was three times face value, close to what I considered a reasonable price. It was at the end of the arena where the Red Wings would be on offense for two of the three periods. There should be a plenty of action from their potent offense, correcting their poor offensive performance in game one. Too few shots had contributed to their 2-1 loss in the opener.

Since I was eager to have my hands on the ticket as soon as possible, and was perhaps more than slightly skeptical of this telephone order (there are flim-flams in the reselling of tickets!) I drove to the address of Ticket King, 15 Ferris Street, as soon as I arrived in the Motor City. After getting lost in a decidedly unsavory part of town, I called the ticket broker for a refresher on the directions, and eventually pulled up to the locked iron gate of a warehouse. When I rang the doorbell, Dennis came out, tied up the Doberman, and invited me into his office to pick up my ticket. All was as advertised. Ticket, price, location, and charge to my credit card were everything he had promised.

Walking to the arena from the Westin Hotel, I joined a growing parking lot crowd at COJO Bob's Bar. A local radio call-in show by WJFN's Magic Man, Michael Stoner, was pumping the crowd. This sports talk show would continue for a couple of hours, and the hosts were trying to generate enthusiasm among the crowd as they entered Joe Louis Arena. Magic Man made a good impression on this out-of-towner with his clean, family-oriented style and enthusiastic delivery.

A sign outside the arena ticket office said "No Resale of Tickets at Any Price on the Arena Premises." However, a few tickets were exchanged and a few offered for sale, high upper level seats. They had an asking price of $275, and one gentleman was asking $300 each for three seats in a suite. I thought for a minute that I may have missed a great deal. But after finding my seat on the first row of Section 213B, I was very satisfied with my ticket strategy and my location. The suite seat would have been at the top of the arena. While decidedly cushy, with convenient bathroom facilities and refreshments close at hand, they were much too far removed from the action.

My seat mates' curiosity soon peaked when they learned I had flown in from Nashville for a single game. A New Jersey Devil fan had occupied the same seat on Saturday, at the same price. Turns out some unknown party owned the single season ticket and sold the seat for each event. After learning that these seats cost $43 per game for a forty-one home-game schedule, plus the requirement to buy the exhibition games, plus $100 per game for the Stanley Cup Championship package, my $300 ticket became more of a bargain, I rationalized.

These Detroit fans could not understand how Nashville could support an NHL franchise. I had the same reservations, but after hearing the crowd and listening to Ms. Karen Neuman's rendition of the national anthem, my appreciation for this sport soared! Here was a game being played in an arena designed and constructed for hockey, with no compromises to accommodate other events. Over nineteen thousand fans with standing-room-only spectators filling Joe Louis Arena made for one of the more memorable sporting spectacles of my life.

The physical contact of the sport, the speed of the skaters, the gritty performances in the corners, the battles at the goal, and yes, even the flying octopus hitting the ice ignited the fervor of the spectators. Their support for their Red Wings told this outsider that a tradition was being honored here tonight, and for two-and-a-half hours the red and white clad Wing fans were totally immersed in their team.

I wondered what was going on in New Jersey and in Nashville. Had I witnessed the eventual Stanley Cup champions being caught in a powerful financial and political struggle? The controversy would be resolved and the outcome known soon enough. But on June 21, 1995, fairness and justice seemed to be best served by rewarding the rich Detroit Red Wing tradition with another Stanley Cup banner — number eight — to hang from the rafters of Joe Louis Arena, and allow the Devils to take the hindmost.

I thought what an irony it would be if the Devils won the Stanley Cup and moved to Nashville next season. A thirty-five-year-old 10,000-seat coliseum awaited them. The new $150 million Nashville Arena, which may eventually cost $160 million, would not be ready for hockey until the 1996-97 season.

As it turned out, the Devils swept the Red Wings in four games. No return to Joe Louis Arena for game five. My premonition that I had to see game two had been correct. The ticket fairy even knows which games to pursue!

As a sports junkie for so many years, my inclination now is to readjust my focus. If college sports can avoid the pitfalls inherent in huge athletic department budgets, then watching the amateurs — the ones who still have a heart for it all — offers the most interest for me.

After seeing sporting events for fifty years, I'm much more sympathetic to those Brooklyn Dodger and New York Giants fans whose teams abandoned them in the '50s for the prospects of growth and a new frontier on the west coast. Life is about coping with change, setbacks, and losses. Our heroes are human, fragile, and flawed with warts when the truth and reality are fully exposed. The owners argue, "It's our money that is at risk. We must make a profit," they exclaim. Today's players seem to consider themselves in the entertainment business, with careers that are short-lived and suspect to an unpredictable end. Their agents argue, "Pay them what they're entitled to during their prime years." Everyone is looking out for their own personal financial interest. Loyalty is replaced with greed. A sport replaced with dollars. The fan's interest finishes last!

You Saw *What*?

Calgary Stampede 1986

Rocky Mountain Yeeee-Hi

My good friend Carl Vorlander talked often about retiring to Kalispell, Montana, and running a service station. As a person who had managed computer services for the state governments of Wisconsin and Minnesota, and later served as executive director of the National Association of State Information Systems, being a pump jockey in the Rockies was his idea of leaving the rat race behind.

With that insight from a savvy ol' Swede in mind, I made Kalispell my entry point for an unforgettable trip. Arriving there via Delta, Ginger and I worked our way through Glacier National Park, Road to the Sun, Prince Edward Park, then back along the west side of the Canadian Rockies to Lake Louise and Banff. If there's more beautiful scenery on earth, I haven't seen it.

In Banff, surrounded by mountains and thick old growth forest, I laid eyes on the Canadian Pacific passenger train passing through town, and it was love at first sight. When I asked about its eastbound schedule, I found I could ride from Banff to Calgary two days later. At the appointed hour, I boarded the observation car for Calgary, with Ginger and Morna following in a rental car. They were waiting

SWZ EC802 233 LEVEL 25 FOUR N M### CHA GRZA1 H 24.00 M 38 13JUN

CALGARY STAMPEDE
CHUCKWAGON RACES &
GRANDSTAND SHOW 8:00 PM
THURSDAY JULY 10, 1986
INCLUDES GATE ADMISSION
14 14 FOURTEEN 14 14
NORTH CLUB M###
N H 38 24.00

Check the back of this ticket for conditions of sale.

at the train station when I arrived. I was like a little kid. What a thrill!

We got to town in plenty of time for the Calgary Stampede. We had ordered tickets to the Chuckwagon Races and the Rodeo, two major events, by mail a couple of months in advance. We had four great seats for the family and a friend Morna had invited along for four days of play.

When we walked in to register at the Palliser Hotel, the lobby was filled with bales of hay; cowboys were everywhere, and the hospitality unbelievable. A Mr. Bill Dickey greeted us in the lobby and thanked us warmly for attending the festivities.

Dickey turned out to be Calgary's great ambassador to us, and made himself indispensable from the first moment we were under his watchful eye. When I gave my reservation information to the clerk, Mr. Dickey asked for an upgrade, which the hotel seemed pleased to do.

After we arrived in the room, a bottle of champagne was sent up along with flowers for Connie Tomlinson, Morna's friend, who would be celebrating her twenty-first birthday that day.

When you're traveling, even if you don't plan to attend a sports event at the time, check out opportunities for future events in the area. The personal touch can make a world of difference in the tickets you get.

Over the next four days, Mr. Dickey served as our personal tour guide to the city, the restaurants, the mass transit, the cowboy entertainment, and tours of magnificent homes on the mesa overlooking the city. Most importantly, after buying us all the obligatory white cowboy hats at the Chamber of Commerce office, he took me to the 1988 Olympic headquarters.

Seated there at the head of the table in the Olympic Committee boardroom, I couldn't help asking, "How can I get tickets to the Olympics in 1988?" Within days after I returned home I would receive ticket applications. I eventually ordered four tickets to twelve events at a total of about $2,600 Canadian, about $2,100 U.S. Four forty-yard-line seats to the Opening and Closing Ceremonies, figure skating championships, pairs figure skating, ski jump, hockey, speed skating, luge, downhill skiing. It was the greatest collection of tickets-for-four that I had ever seen!

But I'm getting ahead of the story. The Stampede had attracted the world's greatest riders for all the rodeo events. For the Chuckwagon Races, they attracted the adventurers. These races are wild and dangerous, with rigs racing around a corral at breakneck speeds. The spectacular spills can injure a horse so badly it has to be destroyed. That part was gruesome, especially with three women in tow.

All the events were held in a state-fair-type setting, complete with squealing pigs racing, rides, amusement park, blue-ribbon bulls, and granny's finest creations. The Calgary Stampede is a great destination for wholesome family fun. Beyond the majestic scenery of the Rockies, the lakes, Banff at midnight, wild animals climbing the hillside, you may be found by a "Ticket Fairy" who will open a new, unexpected world of excitement for one of life's greatest events.

The Queens Tennis Tournament —1989

Wimbledon warm-up

As the Director of Operations, State Headquarters Staff of the Tennessee Air National Guard, I was at Upper Heyford RAF Base in England on a one-week assignment to review the operations of one of our flying units. This unit, the 134th Air Refueling Group, McGhee-Tyson AFB, was there to support the U.S. Air Force Europe and NATO Command, flying KC-135 tankers to refuel European-based F-16s.

Late in the week, two members of the unit invited me to join them for an afternoon of tennis in the London suburbs. Master Sergeant Linda Julian and Senior Master Sergeant Dan Hackney planned to travel by train from Oxbridge to the Queen's Club Tournament. This tournament, sponsored by Stella Artois and known as The Queens, was the warm-up for Wimbledon.

Good friends and the good Lord will take care of you.

We even had a tennis ticket connection. Sergeant Julian's daughter was married to Mike De Palmer, a University of Tennessee tennis player who is now a professional instructor in Florida. One of his teammates was Paul Annacone, then on the professional tour, who was our ticket source for the occasion. Both players have moved up in the world since. As of this writing, Mike coaches Boris Becker, and Paul coaches Pete Sampras.

Paul, his wife, and their baby were all there to greet us. He had been playing in France earlier in the season. The European tour sounds glamorous, but for a family to move from city to city in foreign countries without any roots or stability requires a lot of dedication and grit, especially for the traveling spouse. Nevertheless, they were all upbeat about their lives and Paul's career.

After a chat, Paul excused himself as the rest of us wandered through the huge complex to look for a name player in action, gradually working our way to the clubhouse and center court.

David Frost, the BBC commentator and premier interviewer, was slugging it out in a celebrity singles match with someone we didn't recognize. The inner sanctum, the professional's clubhouse, was home to the greats of tennis, both on the court and off. A buffet luncheon was spread for all to enjoy. We did our part, and then some.

The luxury of moving easily from the dining room to a porch beside center court to watch the name players was as close as I'll ever be to royal tennis. Watching players like Ivan Lendl and Stefan Edberg and others from that vantage point was one of life's treats. All compliments of my friends.

I couldn't have imagined, much less planned, on such a day with the tennis crowd when I left Knoxville at the beginning of the week to visit the 134th Air Refueling Group. One day I was listening to the English air controller at Croughton Airways, flying over the white cliffs of Dover with the controller pointing out historical sites along the southeast coast. The next day, this Tennessee country boy was enjoying lunch in the Queen's Club at center court.

Neapolitan Opera — 1987

Never say never

I've traveled to cities with excellent opera houses. Generally speaking, I wouldn't pay them much mind.

But tell me a performance is sold out and no tickets can be had, and you've got my attention. The chase is on! That was the case in Naples, Italy.

I was serving with a Nashville-based C-130A Air National Guard crew, carrying Lee Greenwood and his troupe on a three-week tour of U.S. military installations around the Mediterranean. Our aircraft commander Bob Doyle, co-pilot Russ Burns, and I had arrived in Naples and were walking down the street when Bob spied the Opera House. His interest in concert halls comes from the fact that in civilian life, he's the manager for country megastar Garth Brooks. We walked to the ticket office to inquire about the evening's performance of the opera, *Norma.* I really had no interest in the opera, but I tagged

along. The show was sold out. Had been for two weeks.

After returning to the hotel from our stroll, I told the guys I would catch up to them later. A sold-out opera in Naples was a challenge I couldn't pass up. I had to find tickets for those two opera-loving buddies. The more I thought about it, the more appeal those multi-tiered European balconies with individual boxes had for me.

I asked the concierge at our hotel if he could find three tickets for that night's opera. "I will check, signore," he replied. About an hour later, he called my room to say he had found three tickets, but not all together. Two were in the loge and one was on the floor, center stage approximately ten rows back. The asking price was affordable, so I instructed him to buy them.

When I walked into Bob's and Russ's room with their pair of loge seats to *Norma*, they were delighted. "The colonel couldn't stand it," they laughed. "He had to accept the challenge!"

While I wouldn't automatically be drawn to an opera in a distant city like I would to a sporting event, the evening proved to be a great experience. Never had I heard an opera performer on stage

Hotel staff can be very efficient when it comes to getting scarce tickets. The manager, concierge, and bell captain probably have local connections and, for a little monetary consideration, will put them to work on your behalf.

booed by an audience! Athletes are quite often booed, but—a baritone? During the first act, the male lead was booed almost on cue, obvious to those who appreciate opera, but certainly not to me. Then, at the conclusion of the first act, as the singers were leaving the stage, he was booed roundly again. Only in Italy!

While the turn-out equaled an attendance record, I am unaware of any other record being broken or tied that evening. It's hard for me to keep score when it comes to operas. Other than the boos, I don't have a clue about the show.

The experience was definitely an adventure, and certainly enhanced Bob's and Russ's opinion of my knack for securing tickets. We enjoy telling that story often.

Since Garth's incredible success, Bob has helped me with tickets for others who wanted to see a Garth Brooks show, as they are always a sell-out. But, I have been to that well only twice. You don't want to have the reputation of abusing a friendship.

Hong Kong Cricket Sixes Championship 1995

Forget the ball, keep your eyes on the bat

In the early autumn of 1995 my wife, daughter, and I were living out a lifelong dream — making a trip around the world. Our first stop westward was Hong Kong. Leaving my wife and daughter to fend for themselves one morning (and foolishly forgetting to confiscate the credit cards), I took a day trip into China to tour a factory making Dockers shoes for Nashville-based Genesco Corporation. When I returned that evening, I told the ladies we had been invited to join my traveling companions for the day — Buzz Davis, Bobby Dale, and former Ambassador to France Joe Rodgers, and their wives, for dinner at the elegant Shangri La Hotel. After a delightful evening on Hong Kong island, we returned to our hotel on Kowloon via the Star Ferry.

Ginger had been picking up brochures during the day, and before we turned in we talked about what to do the next day. I avoid strict schedules when I travel, and organized tours are something that I particularly avoid. I'd much rather plan each day based on the weather and what seems like fun at the time. I usually do this over coffee early in the morning while the women put themselves together. But this evening Ginger, always on the look-out for a sporting event for me, showed me one of her brochures, "Hong Kong — This Week, 29 Sept.-5 Oct. 1995." The Kowloon Cricket Club was hosting nine of the world's top cricketing nations on September 30 and October 1 for the 1995 Cathay Pacific/Wharf Holdings Hong Kong International Cricket Sixes — the only world-class Cricket sixes event anywhere. How could I resist?

The competition, which is for HK $550,000 in total prize money, attracts teams from Australia, England, Holland, Hong Kong, India, New Zealand, South Africa, The West Indies, and Sri Lanka. Each team fields six players per side instead of the usual eleven, hence the name Cricket Sixes. The result is a faster paced, higher scoring game, with matches taking about forty-five minutes to complete in contrast to a traditional match, which can last all day, or several days. This was the fourth consecutive year for the tournament to be held in Hong Kong, and the excitement from the previous years made it one of the Crown Colony's most popular sporting events.

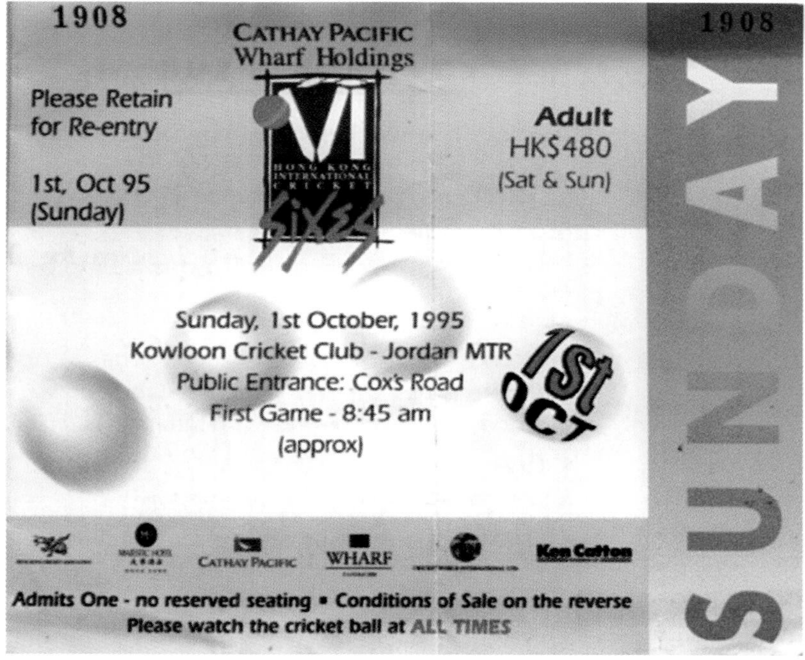

England's squad had won two consecutive championships. Another this year would win them permanent possession of the coveted Golden Bat, which is not only an honor but a trophy valued at nearly HK $800,000 — more than US $100,000.

Competition began with round-robin matches in three groups of three teams each. From each group, the two teams with the best record proceeded to the championship finals.

The matches were on Saturday and Sunday, with tickets for both days priced at HK $480 (US $60) for adults and HK $250 (US $35) for children under sixteen. I opted for the Sunday championship matches only. Once again I would travel alone, while the women enjoyed fabulous Hong Kong shopping.

I arrived at the Kowloon Cricket Club at mid-morning, after a leisurely buffet in the hotel restaurant, only to find the championship matches sold out! I took up the challenge. Not to panic, I walked to the Club Members' Entrance. But I found no activity and no way to get in. I stopped at a gate along side the street where policemen were controlling access to the field, and a couple of plainclothesmen were monitoring the entrance. I asked one of the officers where I might buy a ticket. He suggested, "Just wait around here until someone shows up with an extra." Might work, might not. "Worth a shot," I thought to myself.

Eight or ten young men already were loitering around trying to pick up tickets. Otherwise, everyone who planned to watch the matches was already inside. From the sidewalk entrance, a few feet above the playing area, I could see that the stands were filled on two sides. A third side, across the field from where my entrance was, appeared to be only corporate booths, with umbrella tables to shield the elite from the sun. On the fourth side were more huge umbrellas and casual seating arrangements for easy access to the clubhouse, probably a members-only area.

A car pulled up. A lady got out and announced she had a ticket for sale. Since I was the last to arrive, I waited to see if there was an unofficial pecking order as a courtesy to those who had been waiting. Someone asked, "What do you want for the ticket?" She replied, "$400." I quickly converted that offer from Hong Kong to U.S. dollars. Approximately fifty bucks. That was about twice the face value for a single-day ticket. Doing this mental math, I thought, "That's a decent price. I'm here; it's not prohibitive, and it looks like the only one available." I said, "I'll take it!" No one else had said anything, or even moved. No need to look at the ticket, as all were general admission to the public grandstands on the two sides. The time from her opening offer to sell, to my acceptance and purchase, took ten seconds or less.

The lesson here on ticket purchasing is to know the face value of the ticket, whatever the local currency. If you've done your homework, you can decide as soon as the asking price is announced whether it's worth the money, whether you should hold out for something better, or whether you should make a counter-offer.

Even if the event is a sell-out, lots of tickets are often available, which gives you the luxury of shopping for seat location or price, or both. At the Cricket Sixes, no other tickets were available; it was a sell-out, and the one offer was affordable. Action was the key element.

Once inside the stadium, I stood near a talkative group to try to get some sort of handle on the game of cricket. I still don't understand it, but I do know they hit a lot of balls into the stands, in every direction. What we call a homer in baseball is a "boundary" in cricket, I think. Individual batsmen must retire once their score equals or exceeds thirty-one runs. The Sixes game is unique in that there are only six players on a team and only one inning of five overs each per team. The action is nonstop.

I found the fans and their habits to be as interesting as the cricket matches. As I keep saying, you can never get the same feel for the game on television. Spectators were there from Australia, England, New Zealand, India, and other places I couldn't figure out. The Aussies loved their beers — Carlsberg, Castle, San Miguel, and Sevan lager. Domino's Pizza was for sale. Prommice iced tea and Perrier water were popular, and a vendor, "Let's Do Lunch," was peddling sandwiches.

After all the liquid consumption, the lines to the Port-O-Lets were lengthy. One of the Aussies or New Zealand lads announced, "You need a beer to drink while you're waiting for the toilet." He had finished his beer and still had a long wait in line. Being beerless did not suit him well.

In certain situations, don't think too much about an offer. If you really want in, the ticket is affordable, and no other solution is in sight, buy it!

At halftime the bands, kids, teams, and bagpipers toured the field, entertaining us with music and throwing cricket balls to the crowd. The most inspiring part of the show was the Australian band playing *Waltzing Matilda*.

This break in the action coincided with my pre-set rendezvous time with the women back at the hotel, which was only five or six blocks away. The gate attendant gave me a pass-out, and I told my wife and daughter they must walk back with me to see and feel the atmosphere of the event. The tournament was obviously a great social outing for families, young people, and cricket enthusiasts. For me it was a first; for regular fans it was part of a long and enjoyable tradition.

When the three of us arrived back at the stadium gate, I asked the plain clothes officer, R.E. Smart, General Manager, Guard Force, if he would permit my wife and daughter to enter briefly and take a picture or two. I wanted them to see the crowd, the enthusiasm, and the fun of the outing, and to glance around at the Cricket Club. There was no way to grasp the scope of the game in only a moment, but the atmosphere was a worthwhile experience. Officer Smart graciously let the ladies inside. They thoroughly enjoyed their brief, but unique, exposure to cricket in this international setting. After a few snapshots and soaking in the festive event, the girls were back to the shops within fifteen minutes.

South Africa beat England in the finals that day, denying them the prize of a $100,000 diamond encrusted bat. England missed out despite setting South Africa a target of 82 with two of their batsmen hitting 32 and 31. The South African team steered their way to 86 with three wickets. The latter has something to do with the final result, based on a ratio of runs to wickets. Cricket aficionados will comprehend.

With typical British humor and graciousness the captain for England, Dermot Reeve commented, "South Africa proved better than us in the final. It is disappointing not to win the bat, but at least now I don't have to work out what to do with it."

There will always be an England. Hear, hear!

World Body Board Championship — 1996

Banzai!

Even though I've got my list of all-time favorite sports, I'm always up for championships in interesting events that aren't widely publicized. Especially when I travel, I stay on the lookout for the new and unusual. One winter Ginger and I were on vacation in Hawaii, when I noticed that the tenth World Body Board Championship was being held at the Banzai Pipeline on the north shore of Oahu. The competition ran for nine days, from January 6 to January 14.

Obviously, they couldn't get along without me.

The north side of Oahu is a favorite of my wife's and mine, especially Sunset Beach. We had been there before to enjoy one of our favorite pastimes — watching a beautiful sunset. This time, the spectacle would be man-made. Since I was the only body boarding fan in the group, I drove to the beach alone.

In 1996, for the first time in the fourteen-year history of the event, the Banzai Pipeline winner would not automatically be the world champion. Instead, it would be the final stop on what had become a world tour for competitors in the Global Organization of Body Boarding. (Wonder if they call it GLOBB?) Mike Stewart, the defending world champion and winner of nine previous Pipeline contests, thought the new system was a sign the sport was maturing and being taken more seriously. "We'll finally have a true world champion, instead of having everything riding on one event," he commented to the press.

Brazil's Guilherme Tamega, the 1994 world champion, was the leader after eight stops on the tour. To win his second title, all he had to do was finish third at Oahu. Tamega did finish third and won the world tour crown. But Mike Stewart was the champ at the Banzai Pipeline that day, riding the six- to ten-foot surf to win the Morey Body Board World Championship.

Photographs of the competition make it clear that body boarding itself supplies only part of the total ambiance. The day was like a giant beach party, with music and refreshments a-plenty, and a seemingly endless procession of handsome men and beautiful young ladies struttin' their stuff in the latest (read: itsy-bitsy) swimwear fashions. I caught myself holding in my stomach a couple of times, but I was mostly too fascinated by the skill and bravery of the competitors to worry about anything else.

The sun, the wind, the roar of the breaking surf — everything combined to make it an experience no photograph or TV broadcast could ever capture. In that regard, it's like so many other sporting events, especially outdoor contests. The real world offers much more than even the best wide-screen TV in terms of a view, a feel, a perspective, and, in this case, the beautiful and interesting spectators. No TV means no TV commentators give us the technical analysis or "expert" opinion. In most sports, they can't agree among themselves, so why should I let them get me all confused? I'll gladly trade a gaggle of talking heads to see the excitement live.

Allow me to digress a moment on the subject of TV analysts, who aren't always so reliable anyway. In 1996, after watching eight SEC tournament games in two days, I had been invited for a weekend of golf at Augusta National. I had just sat down on a Delta flight from New Orleans to Atlanta when a noted TV basketball analyst boarded the plane and headed toward a seat across the aisle from me. This Expert Analyst spoke to the gentleman sitting ahead of me and asked, "Are you going to see your conference play basketball?" I couldn't hear the answer, but Mr. Analyst continued to stand in the aisle and proffered, "The SEC talent level is the lowest that I have ever seen."

I think most basketball fans would have agreed that Kentucky was in a class by itself, and that the rest of the Conference was seen as "average." But after the first full weekend of NCAA tournament action, the SEC had four teams in the Sweet 16, each in a different bracket. Two eventually made it to the Final Four. They did awfully well to have the "lowest level" of talent. Maybe it was something in the water.

Sports such as body boarding have not attracted much TV coverage to date, and that means there will be no TV analyst between you and the sounds, sights, and joys of the competition. So much the better.

Faded Glory

World Heavyweight Championship — 1987

Once was enough

One of my earliest memories of sports is listening to the heavyweight championship fight of 1946. Louis and Conn were the warriors. Radio was the medium. Television was still unheard of then on Carter Street in Harriman, Tennessee, but my young imagination filled in all the gaps with visions that eventually proved to be far better than the real thing.

The build up to the Joe Louis/Billy Conn bout created a stir in the neighborhood as big as VE and VJ Day had the year before. It was a warm June 19 evening, the end of nearly the longest day of the year, and the sun was still up when the fight began. I huddled with

RLD HEAVYWEIGHT CHAMPIONSHIPS
IKE TYSON VS. PINKLON THOMAS SOUTH
NY TUCKER VS. JAMES DOUGLAS 13
22925664BB0324 3303B66 CO
LAS VEGAS HILTON 05/01 A
AT MAY 30 1987 4:00PM $0.00 37
OUTDOOR RAINCHECK
SEAT ROW/BOX SEC LOC

the rest of the gang near an open window where a radio blared through the screen, bringing us the action blow by blow from another world light years away. Some of the older guys, the teenagers, knew all the statistics on the two contenders — height, weight, reach, fist size, chest, overall record, knockouts, and who had gone the distance of fifteen rounds. How the oddsmakers used all that to come up with a 3-1 pick boggled our young minds. But we took it all in, picturing the day when we would be there to watch a championship fight in person!

The radio announcer said ringside seats costs up to $100. How could I, as a nine-year-old boy who had never even seen $100 all at the same time, ever imagine witnessing one of those fights? Life is strange. Forty-one years later the setting sun lighted a desert hotel, the scene for a May 30 championship fight. And I would be there to see the undefeated heavyweight champion of the world, Mike Tyson.

When you find yourself out of town with a little extra time on your hands, check to see what sporting events are scheduled locally. Your transportation and hotel are already paid for. Might as well make the most of it.

I was on duty with the Air National Guard, with the good fortune to be in Las Vegas on a Saturday afternoon in May 1987, the day Mike Tyson was to defend his title against Pinklon Thomas. There would be a doubleheader heavyweight championship fight that night. Tyson at 29-0 and Thomas at 29-1 would be battling for the WBA/WBC titles. Tony Tucker, 33-0-1 (1 NC), faced Jim (Buster) Douglas, 23-3-1, for the IBF title. I didn't know about the fight until I arrived at my hotel on The Strip. No one else on the air crew had any interest, so I walked to the Hilton Hotel in search of a ticket, my head filled with memories of a June night in 1946.

In spite of the small seating capacity at the outdoor arena, tickets were available at the box office — the big crowd was the worldwide television audience. There were no bad seats. Ringside had its smattering of movie celebrities, but none impressed me enough to remember their names. The aura of the 1946 radio broadcast had captivated me. But in real life, this so-called "sporting event" lost its glamour in my eyes. The tinsel city and cheesy surroundings robbed boxing of its true sporting flavor — if it actually ever had any. Wild-haired Don King, escorting the reigning heavyweight champion of the world around the ring, further confirmed my view of this parody. However, Mike Tyson's power and prowess were features to admire, even by someone who wasn't much of a boxing fan.

The odds were stacked prohibitively in Tyson's favor, but what would a World Heavyweight Championship fight be without a bit of a wager? The handicappers thought Thomas could withstand Tyson's stiff right for six rounds. Surely Pinky could dance around the ring for six three-minute rounds. Like most every other part of the ambiance that night, it was just another sucker bet. Tyson won a TKO in the sixth round.

As the arena began to clear, I decided this is one sucker who will forego championship boxing in the future. The Louis/Conn fights had seemed so real and believable on the radio. Reading the pre-fight hype, then listening to the punch and parry between two distant warriors had been such a thrill. Those heroes now seemed far away — about as far as Hometown USA from Las Vegas.

Perhaps maturing makes you too skeptical. Or maybe boxing

has changed through the years. My boyhood image of the world heavyweight boxing championship was tarnished by reality. Louis and Conn had been authentic sports heroes to me. Whoever heard of two heavyweight crowns, the WBA/WBC and the IBF? Two fights for two separate titles dilute — not enhance — the tradition. Boxing and Las Vegas have given sports a double-sucker bet.

Thank goodness I'll always have Louis and Conn, and the radio blasting out loud and clear just beyond the screen door.

U.S. Tennis Open — 1994

Better to be a bluffer than bluffed

Quite honestly, I would never have scheduled a trip to Flushing Meadows, New York, to watch a tennis match, even the U.S. Open. I played tennis for a few summers growing up, but never developed the love for it that I had for rival summer sports. Indoor tennis was unknown at that time, and for me summer meant baseball, golf, and the great outdoors.

I had gone to Washington over Labor Day weekend to see the Redskins open their 1994 season, and in particular to see former UT quarterback Heath Shuler make his debut in the NFL. As I was a big Shuler fan and a Redskins fan, I wanted to be there for his first pro game. I'd had Redskins season tickets since 1965, so that little detail was taken care of for once.

At the wedding of my friend Charlie Cornelius earlier that weekend, I told another guest, Major General Charlie Evers (Ret.), that I was thinking of making a side trip from the 'Skins game to see some of the U.S. Open. Since his daughter Linda had attended the University of Tennessee on a tennis scholarship, I thought he might have some advice on getting a U.S. Open ticket. His suggestion was to catch the hotel shuttle from La Guardia to the Marriott across the freeway. From there another shuttle ran to Flushing Meadows. A few years ago, he had asked on the shuttle bus if anyone had an extra ticket, and ended up in the same box with New York mayor Ed Koch.

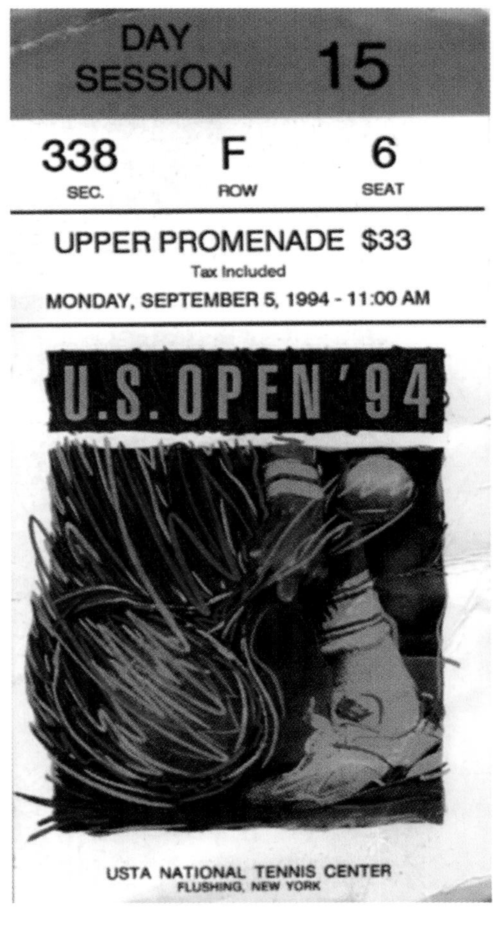

The Delta shuttle goes into the original La Guardia terminal, and my friend Al Brockob, a former Pan Am captain and currently a 767 captain with Delta, told me to take time to soak up the aviation history there, where elegant seaplanes came and went during the earliest years of long-distance air travel. The history of aviation is portrayed around the interior dome of the terminal, from the mythical flights of Central and South American Indians to the Pan American Clipper seaplanes that were the most advanced airliners of the time. You could imagine the well-dressed passengers of the late '30s and early '40s walking out the gate to board their luxurious Boeing 314A. Their Atlantic flight began with a water taxi to the ocean for takeoff. The next morning the Clipper would land in an estuary on the west coast of Ireland. The passengers deplaned at Shannon Airport after being pampered overnight, ready for a steaming cup of Irish coffee.

After this aviation history respite, I boarded a bus to the main La Guardia terminal, then the Marriott shuttle to the hotel, which I could see across the Grand Central Freeway. I first asked the concierge and bell captain if they had access to any tickets. One made a telephone call and said it would be a while before the broker would get back to him. I checked my baggage and went to the restaurant for some breakfast. The hotel was filled with tennis fans, but no one with an extra ticket, nor could any of the hotel staff come up with a single. So as Charlie Evers had suggested, I boarded the shuttle to the tennis venue to try my luck.

When I asked if anyone had an extra, one fellow volunteered one for the night round. Otherwise I received some glaring looks, like, "If you don't have a ticket, why are you on this van?" One attractive lady with a Traverse City sweater talked as if they were annual visitors to the Open. All appeared to be well-to-do, and huge tennis fans. I was there strictly to fill a square on my personal Top Events list.

Dropping us off at the entrance to the Open, the driver announced the return times and pick-up point. I faded into the slow-paced, upper-crust crowd, which was obviously more sophisticated than the throngs at La Guardia, Kennedy, or any sports venue in

New York. Outwardly, they seemed relaxed and ready for an easy, carefree day of tennis. The day was perfect — felt a little like football weather — with a hint of early fall crispness in the air.

I stuck my head in several ticket huddles to get a feel for seat location, availability, and asking prices. Steffi Graf was playing on the center court. After a little scouting, I decided that a ticket to the prime Agassi/Chang match-up would not be a problem. I had time to spare. I relaxed and just walked around, enjoying the unfamiliar yet pleasant ambiance. I went to a bank of telephones to call Ginger and let her know I was about to get this event out of the way and should be home by 11:30 p.m. tonight!

I also had to tell her about what had happened at the Redskins/Seahawks game the day before. By the time I had parked and raced into the stadium, I either forgot to buy a program or the vendors were sold out. After the game I began looking to buy one. No dice. I approached one young couple where the fellow had six or eight programs under his arm, but he wasn't interested in selling one. A couple of women would not part with theirs, even though I offered a premium price.

This happened three or four times before I saw two people dressed in Redskins jerseys, standing at an exit with a young lady. I asked the woman wearing the jersey if she would be willing to sell her program for $10. She looked at her husband quizzically, then back at me, and asked, "Why are you so interested in a program?" I said that I was a UT season ticket holder and a big Heath Shuler fan. I also had Redskin season tickets, and had flown to Washington this morning from Nashville to see Heath's inaugural pro football game. I wanted a program from the game.

She handed it to me and said, "You can have it." I insisted on paying for it. She looked at her husband and smiled. The young lady with them was standing quietly to the side. The light went on. I said, "You are Heath's parents, aren't you? Your name is Joe!" They just smiled modestly. Then we went into one of those wonderful, unexpected, long conversations that makes attendance at live sporting events such a thrill, and proves that not all the drama of a sporting event is on the field.

Joe and Marge Shuler had flown from Los Angeles on the overnight red-eye after watching their other son, Benji, play in a UT loss to UCLA. Now, with Heath's girlfriend, they had watched Heath achieve a lifelong dream. I told Joe B. and Marge Shuler that I had cut out a letter they had sent to the editor of the Nashville *Tennessean* thanking the fans for supporting their son at UT. I had saved their Bryson City address with the intention of writing them to offer the use of my tickets to some of the Redskins' games. I figured that Joe's relatives and friends would be leaning on him for tickets to see Heath play. Probably a cousin would call that they had not heard from since the last family funeral, along with a few folks they didn't even realize were relatives.

This incredibly lucky meeting made the letter unnecessary. Joe was grateful for the use of the tickets, and I was delighted to have these scarce ducats to share with Heath's family. I hope Heath is a Redskin for all his career and that I am able to supply tickets once in a while to someone who genuinely appreciates them.

After telling Ginger the whole tale, I shifted gears back to the tennis crowd and the matter of a ticket for the Agassi/Chang match. One fellow approached me with an inexpensive ticket in Tier III or

C, but once inside I was supposed to go to the Lower Promenade and see his uncle, and for another $30 he would seat me at courtside. Only in New York! I passed on that opportunity. I decided to pay regular price in Section 338 and just watch from there. After all, how bad could the seats be in a stadium that seats only a few thousand?

After strolling around the other courts and getting a feel for the whole complex I visited a few of the vendors' stands. Rather than having huge tents like the Golf Grand Slam events, the vast selection of tennis memorabilia was sold from small individual booths. Since I am not a tennis buff, I bought only a few mementoes. No tennis shirts or things like that. I didn't want to carry them around.

Inside the stadium, I easily found my seat, about six rows from the top in the corner, with lots of room to spread out. I watched the end of the women's match, then paid a visit to the specialty food stands, which were more to my liking than the souvenir stands.The Beautiful People were everywhere, as much to see and be seen as to watch championship tennis.

Perched again on my lofty seat I thought, "If there's a better seat that's still empty, no reason not to move down closer to the action." I walked to a row of seats near a tunnel entrance. From there the number of seats per row increased from one to three to five and upward. I picked the row with three seats. Maybe only a couple would show up. Across the aisle, two women were playing the same seat upgrade maneuver I was, except that they had paid one of the ushers to seat them where they were. Eventually a couple joined me in the row of three.

Caught red-handed, the two women across from me were told to vacate their unauthorized seats. Their pay-off had failed. (Wonder if that was the $30 uncle?) They scurried back into the tunnel to regroup. The Agassi and Chang match was underway by now, and the empty seats had just about disappeared. One of the female duo found a seat close by me and the other approached me and said, "You are in my seat." I was up to the bluff. I said, "I do believe we're both playing the same game. Let me see your ticket." She turned and left. Score one for the Tennessee boy.

Agassi's girlfriend, Brooke Shields, was in the corner at courtside a few rows in front of me with an escort, bodyguard, or whatever. Brooke was taking lots of pictures, and I would assume she was using the brand of camera that her beau was promoting on TV.

At some point I become sated with the lobs, slams, aligning of strings, and tugging at uniforms, and departed for the Marriott van pick-up point. I retraced my steps back to the La Guardia main terminal. A father and son were on the bus. I expect this tournament was an annual outing for them going back to a time when the son was a lot younger. Now, he stepped off the bus at one airline, his father at another. I pondered their somewhat mixed-emotion farewell. It was casual, portraying a matter-of-fact conclusion to a memorable time together. Yet both seemed grateful for the quality time.

We all have our favorite sports, and after attending the U.S. Open, mine are still basketball and golf. Tennis will have to wait for another day.

A grandson or granddaughter with a love for tennis could make a fan out of me. I think back to the father and son at the airport and their warm bonding experience. Some families will find it in baseball, others in playing golf, camping, or something else. Each family has its own unique outlets for sharing time and making memories. I hope the two I saw at La Guardia return for many years to come, and that in good time, there's a grandson to keep the tradition alive.

Belmont Stakes — 1995

The winner in 25 hours

Ever since watching the Kentucky Derby in 1983, I had wanted to see the final and longest leg of the Triple Crown, the Belmont Stakes. I'm not sure what came over me, but as I got near the end of my list of Top 25 sporting events, I decided in 1995 to try to fly to JFK in the morning, attend the Belmont, and get back home that same night. Under normal circumstances the trip would be a piece of cake. The sticky wicket was that the race would start in twenty-five hours!

I called the Belmont track at 2:45 on the Friday before the race, and talked with Reserved Seating. They switched me to the office of Mr. Jerry Davis's office, who I later learned was in charge of admissions and parking. Lorraine Pace in his office was unable to assist me. Back to Reserved Seating. They would not accept a credit card. Back to Lorraine Pace. I asked her, "Will you trust me?" I told her I was arriving on a Delta flight at 12:30 tomorrow afternoon, race day. She put me on hold, then came back on the line to say, "We'll hold a ticket until 1:30 tomorrow." I asked for 1:45, leaving me an hour to get to the track from the airport, both of which are on Long Island. "That is no problem. Come to the third floor of the clubhouse when you arrive."

By 3:15 Friday I had plane tickets, clubhouse tickets, and had been advised that a taxi was the only way to travel from JFK to Belmont. A 12:30 arrival and a 7:45 departure gave me ample time to see several races before the ninth — the Belmont Stakes — and return to JFK.

Time for a little quick research. A trip to the downtown Nashville library at 3:15 produced an excellent horse racing book, *Winning at the Track*, by David L. Christopher (Liberty Publishing Company, Deerfield, Florida, 1st ed., June 1983). This prominent Baltimore businessman writes under several pseudonyms to avoid attracting attention to his pastime. He developed his betting system while in college, and stated early on in the book that it was intended strictly as an enjoyable hobby. "Money should only be a means of keeping score." My granddaughter Zara accompanied me to the library, which meant the biggest part of our time was spent in the children's section on the second floor. The marionettes and other diversions were at least as exciting for her as handicapping horses was for me.

I left Nashville the next morning at 7:30, arriving at JFK on time at 12:30. The estimated JFK-to-Belmont fare given by the NYC taxi dispatcher was $15. As soon as we pulled from the airport curb, however, the cabbie informed me, "It will be double the meter. I can't bring a fare back from Nassau County." Or so the story went.

We got to talking. The cabbie had been a jockey in Trinidad at age seventeen. He was fifty-six now and had been in New York thirty-two years. Down on his luck. He told me about his days as a jockey, and how he and his competitors had had to let certain jockeys win, or else they would be severely beaten. In Trinidad he said there were no starting gates, only a rope. The horses would walk outbound from the rope and only then would the other jockeys tell him who was to win this race. This allowed the pre-selected winner to get a favorable starting position. He said that his trainer asked him on several occasions why he didn't hit an opening gap at some point when he had a chance to move up in the pack. According to James, none of the jockeys could reveal the jockeys' secret. After they mounted their horses, only the jockeys knew who would win. But whoever it was, they always spread the wealth around.

The cabbie decided he had a Major Player in his back seat. He said, "Nobody flies to New York City just to go to the Belmont Park without knowing something." When I said "I'm just a sports fan interested in seeing the Belmont Stakes," he said, "You're a modest man." Did I own a horse? What was my interest in the day's race? I was unable to convince him of my true identity. Finally, he insisted on knowing which horse I was going to bet. I told him Thunder Gulch, with Wild Syn as my long shot. "Why Wild Syn?" he asked. I remembered that Wild Syn led the Kentucky Bluegrass Stakes wire-to-wire. With that he said, "I'll put $2 on that horse." I told him, "By 6 p.m. you'll know that the guy from Nashville was really who he said he was and nothing more."

Security called Ms. Pace from the clubhouse gate to verify my identity and sent me to Jerry Davis's third floor office. Ms. Pace personally escorted me to Row B, Seat 8 in 3J. The winner's circle was immediately below me, and ABC's Al Michaels was there for the pre-race introductions. The Ticket Fairy lives.

On the flight from Nashville, I had read the handicapping method employed by Mr. Christopher. After entering the clubhouse and collecting a program, the Daily Racing Form, and a felt-tip pen with "127th Belmont Stakes" in green on ecru, I was prepared for the next three-and-a-half hours of racing. I had missed the first three races and started handicapping the fourth. I bet a $2 quinella on the #3 and #6 horses, and a $2 show ticket on the #7 horse. Evil Bear #3 and Corona #6 finished 1-2. I should have bet the exacta, but I cashed a $6.50 ticket.

I was busy handicapping the sixth race with ten entries and three eligibles when the knowledgeable trackster next to me volunteered, "The #2 and #5 horses have been scratched." My shortcomings on handicapping horses were even worse that I had thought. I was prepared to bet on a horse that wasn't even running.

Next came lunch in the clubhouse deli, and time to apply my system for the Stakes race. The first three horses had insufficient racing history to handicap them. Using Christopher's method, I had Thunder Gulch at 309 points, Composite at 308 points, and Star Standard at 291. I liked Star Standard's granddad, Secretariat, so that was worth another $2 Win-Place ticket. Wild Syn was in the 280s, but that was my long shot. So, my triple was 10-6-12 for $2, and $10 across-the-board on Thunder Gulch.

With my betting completed I could go to the paddock to see the horses, jockeys, ladies' fancy hats, owners, and wannabes. I thought, "With all the money these owners have, I suppose entering a Triple Crown race is a small price to pay for all the excitement and pizzazz." For those of us who are worlds apart from this setting, these excesses should be sniffed, not swallowed whole. I'm grateful for having been in that beautiful park. It was like being in a fairy tale.

After Thunder Gulch clinched the victory, I enjoyed all the post-race festivities from my perch. The winning horse and jockey, as well as trainer Wayne Lucas, were duly ecstatic with winning the third race of the Triple Crown.

As I was leaving, I discovered that I had lost my admission-ticket stub, but still had my stick-on clubhouse lapel tag. I approached a white-haired gentleman who was wearing a paddock label on his lapel and asked, "Do you still have your ticket stub?" I might as well have said, "Quick, do you know the cube root of 10,010?" "No!" he barked. "Do you have yours?"

It was like an exchange from Ayn Rand's *Atlas Shrugged.* He obviously was a person of wealth and prestige, and enjoyed his own personal power. He never understood my explanation. "I have lost my stub and wanted to keep one for a souvenir." A young lady, probably his daughter, walked up about this time and explained to him, "He wants a ticket stub." Then she remembered, "We were admitted on a pass."

The old gentleman was going to have the last word, as I presume he was accustomed to doing. "Here," he said, throwing his losing pari-mutuel tickets on the ground. "Is this what you want?" He stormed off into his world, and I into mine. I cashed my Belmont Stakes tickets for $68.10. My wagers had totaled $44, and I tipped the red-headed Irish lass at the pari-mutuel window $5 for a bit of Irish luck. My net for the 127th Belmont Stakes was $19.10.

Ms. Lorraine Pace in Jerry Davis's office at Belmont had made my day. Only twenty-five hours before one of the most famous races in the world, she graciously found a premium ticket for a total stranger. I found the hospitality at Belmont Park in New York every bit the equal to what I'd expect in the South. The management could not have been nicer. Later in the racing season, Ms. Pace forwarded the application for the Breeders' Cup to me. I had a conflict with a college football game, but I hope to save that pleasure for another time.

Returning home to Nashville where my granddaughter Zara awaited, I savored the good fortune of seeing the next-to-last event on my list of Top 25 Sporting Events.

As I run out of worlds to conquer in sports, I am transferring that energy to story time at the library, bird-banding at the local park, and other pursuits with a wide-eyed five-year-old who's become my new inspiration.

Up and Coming

U.S. Open Women's Golf — 1980

Hometown heroines

When a major sporting event comes to your hometown, it does away with a lot of the challenges of the chase. You don't need transportation or hotels, and you can get tickets on your lunch hour. Then all you have to do is show up at the gate.

That was the scene in 1980 when the LPGA's U.S. Open came to the old Richland Country Club in Nashville. This beautiful downtown club later succumbed to urban progress, replaced by a new Jack Nicklaus-designed course at the county's edge. But at old Richland during one broiling July week in 1980, the best in women's golf was center stage in Music City.

Quite honestly, had the tournament been held some distance away, I probably would have skipped it. But the best in their sport were playing for the most prestigious cup in women's golf. It was a sport that was on the rise, steadily attracting more media attention and more prize money. I wanted to take advantage of this home-grown opportunity.

Don't overlook local sporting events. It's easy to ignore them, especially if they're on television. But your local promoters deserve your support. Besides, it's a lot more fun than sitting on the couch.

I also wanted to see how far the women could hit the ball. Since I played that course once or twice a year, I could compare my distances to theirs. This was a first for me, playing the same course that also hosted a women's golf tournament. Augusta was the only other course I had ever played where the pros also played.

Though I wouldn't have expected it, watching the women practice alerted me to many shortcomings in my own game. Amy Wolcott practiced a drill that got my attention quickly. Her caddie set up a garbage can off to the side of the practice area. From varying distances of perhaps seven to twenty yards, Amy began to hit soft wedge shots toward the can, with a fair percentage landing inside. She was impressive! Little did I know at the time that I was watching the eventual U.S. Women's Open Champion.

Beth Daniels, Joan Carner, Nancy Lopez, and Pat Bradley were a few of the popular golfers at the tournament, and any one of them could have been the winner. One petite blonde who probably could not win but might make the cut was a crowd favorite named Laurie

Baugh. She was from Cocoa, Florida, and had been taught by her father from a young age. My friend Dan Ballew, who lived in Cocoa Beach, told me about her and said to be sure to follow her for a few holes. She was a pleasure to see — an easy, natural swing, not an extremely long hitter, but competitive.

As the heat was between the high nineties and one-hundred degrees with humidity like only Tennessee can have, it was like a steam bath out there. The players were more durable than the fans. Two days were enough for me. I don't think Ms. Baugh made the cut for the final two days either.

When many of these same women players returned to Nashville eight years later for the Sara Lee Golf Classic at the nearby Hermitage Golf Course, I went to watch them in an early May setting. This time the heat wasn't the culprit; the rain was. I saw Laura Baugh again, surrounded now by attractive little blonde-headed children rushing to their mother after every round.

Amy Wolcott plays in the Sara Lee Classic occasionally and continues to win her share on the tour. As of this writing, she needs one more win to reach the threshold for admission to the LPGA Hall of Fame. If her pitching game stays like it was in 1980 when I saw her lobbing shots into that garbage can, my bet is she'll have her thirtieth tour victory by the time you read this.

Brickyard 400 — 1994

Instant winner

How did a first-time sporting event make it onto my list of favorites? The Brickyard 400 is absolutely unique, combining the grand traditions of Indianapolis with the fastest-growing spectator sport in America, NASCAR racing. Stock car entries running on the most famous car track in the country came only after a long list of hide-bound rules and traditions were finally removed in 1994.

The Indy auto races date back to 1911. NASCAR racing began on the big track in 1949. Indianapolis Motor Speedway with its flat, perfectly elliptical two-and-a-half-mile course, originally paved with brick, was the home of Indy-type cars that appealed to a full range of followers — everyone from the proper and sophisticated fans who occupied the box seats under the covered deck, to the wild uncontrollable anything-goes crowd that dominated the infield. The nation tuned in on the radio to hear of Bill Vukovich, A.J. Foyt, Parnelli Jones, or Mauri Rose taking the checkered flag. For all the excitement on the track, the happenings in the infield are worth the price of admission. A crowd approaching 400,000 flocks to the Brickyard every Memorial Day.

The NASCAR circuit grew out of stock car races held on dirt tracks of varying lengths and shapes. The crowds loved the banging, slamming, and devil-may-care driving habits of those daring drivers. As the NASCAR following grew and the tracks improved, entrepreneurs saw the potential in this fledging new breed of drivers. Each weekend brought a new venue and, some would say, "The Bubba throng."

After about thirty years of being ignored beyond their Southern roots, NASCAR emerged with a nationwide following and a bulging bank account. The likes of Coach Joe Gibbs left the world of Super Bowl Champions to pursue another challenge — owning his own racing team. You've got to give credit to the family and owner of the Speedway for their vision of a natural event: bringing the big cars of NASCAR to Indianapolis.

Those who held renewable tickets to the Indy 500 in May had the first option on tickets for the first ever Brickyard 400. Ray Woodson and I, along with our wives, had traveled together to our first and

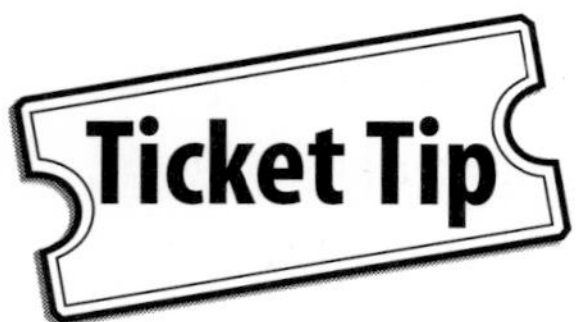

Regular or season ticket holders at a particular sports venue often have ticket priority for new events at that location. Check it out.

only Indy, the rained-out race in 1986. Ray continued to buy Indy 500 tickets each year, and he gradually upgraded his seats. For the inaugural Brickyard 400, he ordered tickets and invited three of his Air Guard buddies to join him. The four of us sat in Stand B, Box 16, Row Y, between the start/finish line and the first turn.

General Fred Womack, Colonel Ray Woodson, Lieutenant Colonel Richard Julian, and I traveled in Ray's new van, making us "Bubbas on the road" for sure. A Louisville hotel was the closest room we could find. The race was sold out early, insuring a crowd estimated at 350,000. Actual race attendance is not released, but a local vendor told me this one had a hundred-million-dollar economic impact on Indianapolis. With coolers conveniently at hand, we watched history being made with the big cars, big engines, and talented drivers attacking this flat track, a departure from the sharply banked turns of Talledega, Darlington, and Bristol.

The checkered flag was waved that day for the crowd favorite, a home town Hoosier by the name of Jeff Gordon. Jeff grew up only a few miles west of Indianapolis, and as of this writing has won nine NASCAR events and captured the Winston Cup Championship for the 1995 racing season. Wonder what he'll do next year when he's twenty-five?

Attracting over 300,000 fans for an inaugural event is a fair indication of NASCAR's popularity. Of course other NASCAR races have more tradition, more long-time supporters, and more dollars invested, and those races will continue to hold the hearts and imaginations of racing fans. With salutes to Daytona, the most popular; to Darlington, the oldest; to Charlotte, the longest race at 600 miles; to Talledega, Atlanta, Dover, Bristol, and others, I believe the Brickyard 400 will be a statement that all NASCAR fans can support and endorse.

Two great racing traditions were brought together by Speedway President Tony George and NASCAR President Bill France. They accomplished something neither the Rose Bowl, the Super Bowl, the Stanley Cup Championship, nor the World Series could accomplish — instant success.

College World Series — 1995

All for love

Before June 5, 1995, I never had any particular urge to see the College World Series. It's a far cry from the classic events that typically attract my attention. But it turns out to be one of the last events where the sheer joy of competition and love of the game hasn't been obliterated by glitz, merchandising, and the posturing of petulant millionaires. Part of the lure of championship college baseball may also be a subconscious need to fill the void created by the major league strike and the cancelled World Series of '94.

In the spring of 1995, I went to two UT/South Carolina baseball games, UT/Vandy in Nashville, and the SEC Tournament in Knoxville. I scarcely attended that many school games when I was a student at UT. The new Lindsey Nelson Stadium on the Tennessee campus was part of the attraction, and I suspect similar classy, modern facilities have continued to spring up around collegiate baseball at Oklahoma State, Tulsa, Miami, Florida State, Clemson, Arizona State, Auburn, and on and on.

The atmosphere in the grandstand around a college diamond is simply unbeatable. Where else can you see head-first slides into first base? Or a pitcher sprinting from the dugout to the mound, and sprinting off again after retiring the side? Or watch 170-pound infielders slam opposite-field home runs with the unaccustomed thwack of an aluminum bat?

You can enjoy a game without a beer, a guy dressed like a chicken, waterfalls, fireworks, or glitzy scoreboards — without outfield walls plastered with every logo known to man. I hope the NCAA does not bow to the temptation to hold this World Series in Dodger Stadium or some domed stadium. How great it is to go to this Series and sit next to average fans. The only celebrity in sight at the '95 Series was Kevin Costner, and he stayed in the Cal State-Fullerton dugout. He was there to support his alma mater. Great!

You won't find scalping of tickets for $300, or up to $1,500 for choice seats. You sit behind your team's dugout for $7.50. Look around and you can see parents, girlfriends, and wives of the players. Their young toddlers are scampering about, and Grandpa and Aunt Meg came to share in the excitement. You visit and talk to these fans; you don't play one upsmanship with questions like, " How did you get your tickets?" At the local restaurants you join parents, athletes, coaches, girlfriends, and friends from opposing teams. Everyone knows baseball. Appreciates baseball. Loves baseball.

I knew Tennessee was going to Omaha, but I didn't know when they would play. On a Wednesday morning I learned they would

play Saturday night against Clemson, a team that had defeated them twice in the regular season. My friend Sam Bartholomew had a daughter who dated the ace of the Vol pitching staff, R.A. Dickey, a graduate of Montgomery Bell Academy in Nashville. Sam wasn't making the trip, but his daughter Ann was going with R.A.'s parents. A call to Southwest Airlines turned up a Friday evening flight. A call to Offutt AFB in Omaha produced a room. A call to Budget Auto Rental produced a weekend rate on a car.

With the basics covered, the next task was finding a traveling buddy. With my best persuasive talents engaged, I telephoned Randy Roberts, my new pal who represented Rawlings Sporting Goods. He was tempted right off. "I'll call you back." Within thirty minutes he called to say TWA had seats on a Saturday morning flight from Nashville to Omaha for $267 round trip. A return flight was available at 6:05 p.m. If UT won the first game, they played on Monday afternoon at 2:30. A perfect fit! I changed my reservations as required, meaning everything was in hand except tickets. A minor detail.

By 3:15 Saturday afternoon, we were at Embassy Suites, the UT headquarters in Omaha, to check on tickets. Since Randy, through his firm Sports Distributors Inc., had sold equipment to the Vols, including some new Rawlings gear especially for the World Series, he knew coaches who could steer us toward some tickets.

As a back-up plan I called Rosenblatt Stadium and placed an order through TicketMaster — two box seats on the right field line for $8.50 each, to be picked up an hour prior to the game at will-call. All was set.

While we were strolling in the hotel lobby, we noticed a father/son duo talking with R.A. Dickey. After R.A. departed, I asked the father, "Do you have tickets?" They were to pick theirs up at the same time we were and needed a ride to the stadium. When I asked if they wanted to get a steak first (after all, we were in Omaha) they were quick to agree. Little did I know that this chance meeting, and inviting Mr. Richard Cummins and Richard Cummins, Jr., to join us for dinner would add immensely to the adventure of three days in Omaha.

On the drive to Rosenblatt Stadium I detected a familiar voice from Richard Senior that had not registered during dinner. I asked, "Richard, do you sometimes call into *Sports Scene* on WLAC?" I watched him and Richard Junior in the rear view mirror. Junior looked at Dad like, "What are you going to tell this guy?" Then, Richard Sr. said, " I call in from time to time." With that Randy said, "You're Gil!" Well, the cat was out. We had "Gil from Green Hills" with us. This guy not only was famous on WLAC radio in Nashville, but also the rival sports talk show on WWTN referred to him as the "Stat Man." Richard Senior is the most knowledgeable and the most articulate caller to either show. And that's not just my opinion, but the view of most of the regular listeners.

For those unfamiliar with *Sports Scene*, it reaches twenty-eight states, Canada, and Mexico between 5 p.m. and 9 p.m. on WLAC-1510 AM. Bob Bell and Bill King are the co-hosts, with coach Doug Matthews assisting on many evenings. While some accuse the show of harboring a Tennessee Vol bias, these broadcasters do a professional and entertaining job, and their knowledge and recall is enormous. The rival WWTN show is at 99.7 FM from 4 p.m. to 7 p.m. Some would argue a Vanderbilt bias there. George Plaster — the voice of the Vanderbilt Commodores — along with Will Daunic and Al Dorsey are sometimes accompanied by Joe Biddle, sports editor of the *Nashville Banner*.

We got to the stadium and found our seats. In the top of the first inning, UT versus Clemson, the second batter up was switch-hitting Scott Schroeffel. His parents from Allison Park, Pennsylvania, his granddad, and his aunt were sitting behind us on row 9, behind the Vol dugout. When Scott hit the pitch over the left centerfield wall and was trotting the bases, I turned to congratulate his parents. Scott's mother beamed with joy through her tears. In front of us were the parents of third baseman Scott Vieira from San Ramon, California, and his girlfriend or wife. To our right were Mrs. Rod Delmonico, wife of the head coach, with her parents from New Jersey and their three sons who wandered from their seats to the top of the dugout, and then to the on-deck circle in the pre-game. Todd Helton, the Colorado Rockies first-round draft pick and number eight in the overall draft, pitched a beautiful four-hitter to beat Clemson 3-1. What fun!

Sunday we drove over to Lincoln to visit Memorial Stadium, home of the 1994 National Football Champions, the Nebraska Cornhuskers. The gate was open to drive under the stadium, but no one was around. I drove our red rental Jeep through the open gates to the edge of the artificial turf. To the dismay of Randy and Richard Senior, I stopped short of driving on the field. I'm sure Coach Osborne would have granted leniency in any penalty, since it was a "Big Red" 4 X 4. After taking pictures on the field, we drove to Misty's, a sports bar/steakhouse in the Lincoln suburbs. There we enjoyed a little taste of the nostalgia served up with an outstanding collection of sports memorabilia.

Monday afternoon, a great Cal State-Fullerton team overwhelmed the Vol ace R.A. Dickey, 11-1. I sat with R.A.'s girlfriend for part of the game and in front of his dad, Harry Dickey, until Randy and I had to leave in the eighth inning to catch our 6:05 flight. R.A.'s dad was very philosophical about the pounding — no regrets, no blames, no excuses. "You're going to have games like this," he mused. I knew he hurt for his son, but that's baseball. In fact, that's life. One day it's chicken, the next day it's feathers.

Win or lose, nothing could detract from the three-day outing at Omaha and the College World Series. In the future I hope progress, overpowering institutions, and long green do not spoil one of the best-kept secrets in sports. My advice: See it quick, before the "bigger is better" syndrome tarnishes this college jewel in Omaha.

The Cream of the Crop

Olympics — 1960, '84, '88, '96

It's easier than you think

The "Games" are the most famous sporting events in the world. But many people don't realize that tickets to the Olympics are not that hard to get. I suspect lots of fans assume there's no way they could ever see the Olympics in person, so they don't even try. While certain events such as Opening and Closing Ceremonies, figure skating, diving, and basketball are tough, plenty of other tickets are inexpensive and plentiful.

In 1996, soccer tickets and baseball tickets were plentiful at the Summer Games in Atlanta. Cycling, field hockey, rowing, and other sports had tickets to spare. While they aren't as popular, these events still give you a taste of world-class competition, and a chance to savor the Olympic experience in person. Besides, you can shop for other tickets after you get there.

When I was growing up, the Winter Olympics were something that took place somewhere far away in the cold, mountainous terrain of Norway or the Swiss Alps, where I assumed people lived in gingerbread houses and rode reindeer to the supermarket. The athletes of Europe dominated winter sports then, from the power of their hockey players and downhill skiers to the finesse and grace of the figure skaters, the most famous of whom was Sonja Henie, the beautiful Swedish figure skater who later became an American movie star.

But in 1960, the Winter Olympics came right into our back yard. High in the Sierras, a little gambling town on the south end of a beautiful glassy lake became a stage for the world's best winter athletes. Lake Tahoe, California, would never be the same. Its anonymity as a quiet retreat for Californians would be lost forever. The cost of waterfront property on Lake Tahoe suddenly skyrocketed. Today it's completely unaffordable, if you can find anybody who'll even talk about selling.

Other Olympic host locales have experienced similar explosions in their property value, and even in their national status. Prior to 1964, Japan was a defeated nation, both in their own eyes and in the eyes of developed nations of the world. As building began for the Summer Games that year, a long dormant pride began to emerge. During my Air Force tour in Japan then, I saw new freeways rising above the antiquated roadways, stadiums under construction, and billboards with word of the world coming to Tokyo in the name of peace. The victors in this battle would win based on performance, not firepower.

By contrast, the Winter Games are usually centered around a remote, quaint village. Even after worldwide exposure, change at a local level has been difficult for some Olympic venues because of their isolation. Lake Placid, Albertville, and Lillehammer all reverted to their former status as winter sports destinations, with pin sales, ice rinks, and ski jumps as the most visible reminders of the fanfare and extravaganza during two weeks in February when the world came to their doorstep.

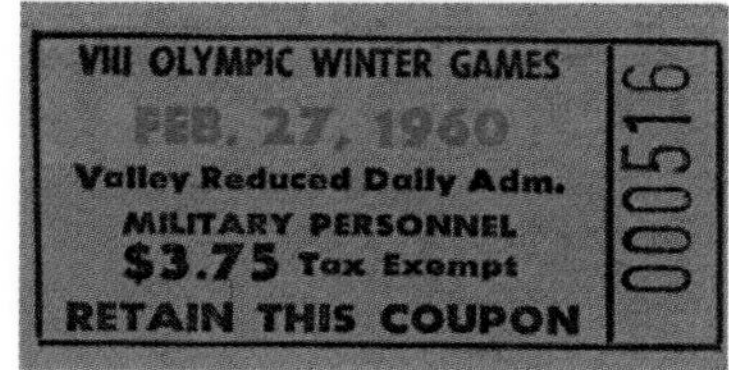
VIII OLYMPIC WINTER GAMES
FEB. 27, 1960
Valley Reduced Daily Adm.
MILITARY PERSONNEL
$3.75 Tax Exempt
RETAIN THIS COUPON
000516

In fact, when I returned to Lake Tahoe in 1990, I was unable to pinpoint that beautiful sunlit deck outside a restaurant where the celebrities had gathered thirty years before to work on their winter tans, Walter Cronkite being one of the more notable persons absorbing those high-altitude ultraviolet rays. The practice rink that the figure skaters had used was only a fond memory. I remembered how Carol Hess caught my attention, even secret admiration, with her winning smile and svelte figure as she displayed her medal-winning skills on the ice. Ms. Hess had been generous enough to interrupt her concentration to flash that winsome smile for a few of us gawkers at rink's edge. That beautiful, blue-sky Saturday in February 1960 is a memory I'll always be grateful for.

But the most incredible, unforgettable event of that long ago day turned out to be one of the most historic events in Winter Olympic history. The USA hockey team upset the highly favored USSR team 3-2. The howling, partisan crowd will long remember that triumphant day for Old Glory.

The San Francisco Chronicle had warned potential spectators that tickets to the battle of the Cold War giants were going for $50 each — an unheard of ticket price in 1960. My traveling companions, Bob Frazier and Bob Anania, were not inclined to pay such a price for a hockey ticket. Natives of Oklahoma and Florida failed to see the sanity of paying that amount of money for an ice-skating battle. Maybe a rodeo or jai-alai event would separate these fellows from fifteen percent of a month's earnings. Not guys skating with sticks.

I wanted to see this once-in-a-lifetime match-up, though. I had never seen a hockey game, not even on TV. The entrance to the ice arena was a huge wall of glass extending to the roof, with a series of double doors using slow-moving pneumatic closers. With so many entrances, admission lines were short to non-existent, even though it was a sold-out event.

People were sitting in the aisles, standing in the back, and packed to the rafters. The noise was deafening. I knew nothing of the rules, the game, nor the players. Yet when they played *The Star Spangled Banner* I knew that I had witnessed the most thrilling sports event of my young life. I can thank a ticket taker for admitting me through one of those slow-to-close doors and becoming part of the crowd.

History would repeat itself at Lake Placid twenty years later before a TV audience of hundreds of millions.

Los Angeles — 1984

My second trip to the Olympics wasn't until 1984, and it was very much a spur-of-the-moment decision. Well-meaning friends will tell you that you have to plan your Olympic visit months or years in advance. For me, this experience proved otherwise. That weekend in the summer of 1984, I became The Couch Potato That Roared.

It's what happens when one moment you're sitting quietly at

Games of the XXIIIrd Olympiad Los Angeles 1984

Day	Date	Time	Price	Event
Thu	Aug 9	9:30 AM	$45	Track and Field
Area	**Section**	**Row**	**Seat**	**Location**
	18	7	7	LA Memorial Coliseum

Issued To
CARL C KOBELT

home minding your business and perfectly happy with the world, and the next moment, you're putting an unanticipated adventure together.

The Los Angeles Olympics in 1984 was a flash like that for me, and in some ways it was one of the best trips I've ever made. I didn't have time to worry about details, so I didn't.

I was at home in Nashville, sitting on the couch, watching the first week of the Olympics on television. The National Anthem was playing, and a young woman from West Virginia who had captured the hearts of America was humbly awaiting her gold medal in gymnastics. Mary Lou Retton, less than five feet tall, was as big as they come in the world of competition.

I hollered into the next room, "Ginger, we're going to Los Angeles."

I had never been to Los Angeles before, but I knew we were up to the challenge. I had to be in Kansas City for a meeting that would conclude on Wednesday. Instead of flying home, I flew west. Even with the Olympics already underway, I had no trouble getting a hotel room or a rental car. And with my track record at getting tickets, I didn't worry about that little detail either.

When Ginger and I got to the Coliseum, driving directly from the airport, the decathlon was in progress. Tickets were bountiful on the sidewalk outside the stadium, and we got inside in time to watch Daly Thompson of Great Britain in five events. He ultimately emerged victorious after the 1500-meter run at the end of a grueling day.

Keep up the the chase, even if you have to leave home without tickets in hand. It takes some guts, and maybe reaching for some of that stashed cash you have put away for a rainy day, but that's all part of the adventure.

We sat on Row 7 near the action, mopping our brows in the heat, with me wishing I'd worn shorts like all the Californians had done. We had an excellent view of the pole vault and discus, both staged in the infield, and could literally feel the tension and excitement among the Brits, Germans, and other competitors.

That night at the Marriott, I developed a plan for getting tickets to events over the last three days of Olympic competition. The USA had fielded strong teams in basketball, volleyball, and diving. I wanted all of those. And of course I wanted to see the closing ceremonies, which would be a tough ticket even with a stadium capacity of 100,000.

We got tickets outside the Forum for the men's basketball championship game and sat about fifteen rows back in the corner of the end zone as the Americans locked up the gold. As Nashville residents, we were particularly interested in watching Vanderbilt coach C.M. Newton assist Bobby Knight in leading the team, and seeing Jeff Turner in action on the court. The playing of the National Anthem at the awards ceremony stirred me even more than it had when I was watching Mary Lou's moment of triumph from my couch!

Volleyball was another straightforward ticket purchase, this time in Long Beach immediately before the game. The price was high, but worth it, since it was the gold-medal round and the USA was playing. Inside, my wife kept asking to use my binoculars. I hadn't known her to be such a keen observer of volleyball technique in the past. Soon I discovered that she was not watching serves, volleys, and spikes at all, but was keeping a close eye on Tom Selleck and his companion on the other side of the arena.

Games of the XXIIIrd Olympiad Los Angeles 1984 114138452

Day	Date	Time	Price	Event
Fri	Aug 10	7:00 PM	$95	Basketball
Area	**Section**	**Row**	**Seat**	**Location**
LOGE	3	D	1	Forum

Issued To
WALTER J NASH

It was the first competitive volleyball either Ginger or I had seen, and we were not disappointed. After the gold medal presentation to the USA team, I turned to her and said, "I've got to hold one of those." We walked to the corridor that led from the arena to the dressing rooms. One of the players was chatting with a young lady in the hall, his medal hanging from a ribbon around his neck. With nothing to lose, I approached and asked whether I might be allowed to hold the gold. He handed it over, beaming with pride. It was large in my palm, cool to the touch, and surprisingly heavy. Though weighty in my hand, it seemed light as a cloud on his chest when I returned it with enthusiastic thanks.

Games of the XXIIIrd Olympiad Los Angeles 1984 114743976

Day	Date	Time	Price	Event
Sat	Aug 11	6:30 PM	$25	Volleyball
Area	**Section**	**Row**	**Seat**	**Location**
BALCONY	224	P	10	Long Beach Arena

Issued To

MARY J THOMPSON

Tickets to the closing ceremony were still proving elusive. Each day I returned to a particular vendor at the Ticket Exchange to see if his asking price had fallen. No such luck. He read me well, deducing from my southern accent and repeated visits to the Exchange that I had come a long way to see the Olympics, and that I wanted those tickets BAD.

"Come on! Buy 'em!" he said. "It's a once-in-a-lifetime opportunity." Then he played his trump. "A year from now you won't miss the money, but you'll sure miss not having been there." His $225 per ticket price was unshakable. Finally on Friday afternoon, I gave in. He had won the stand-off this time, but now I was assured of participating live from Row 9 in an event hundreds of millions of people would be watching at home on television. Without heeding the urge, I would have been one of those poor couch potatoes!

Because I had to be at work the morning after the Closing Ceremonies, I made a dry run from my pre-selected parking spot at the stadium to the car rental return at the airport, adding time for the shuttle to the terminal, baggage check, and security. Then I backed up to the time I would have to leave my seat during the closing ceremonies to catch the red-eye flight to Nashville.

Despite having to leave a few minutes before it was all over, the Closing Ceremonies were the highlight of my four-day adventure in Los Angeles. All those proud young athletes entering the Coliseum bearing their national flags! In the Opening Ceremonies the participants had been organized into national teams. Now they were commingled as ambassadors of the world, a tradition that had begun at the Melbourne Games in 1956.

But then, the whole thing fell apart! I think the Aussies started it, and in a heartbeat a spontaneous eruption of pent-up joy turned a colorful yet somber ceremony into the world's largest yard party! For them it was the fulfillment of a lifelong dream to participate in the greatest amateur athletic competition in the world. A plea came from the loudspeaker over and over, "Will the athletes please return to the middle of the field." And in some small way, I had shared their experience with them, live in person. It was certainly a long way from the living room couch I'd been sitting on nine days before.

With time to spare at my departure gate, I bought a few Olympic pins to add to the hundreds I'd picked up here and there, and a

Games of the XXIIIrd Olympiad Los Angeles 1984 113055863

Day	Date	Time	Price	Event
Sun	Aug 12	6:30 PM	$100	Closing Ceremony
Area	Section	Row	Seat	Location
	14	9	1	LA Memorial Coliseum

Issued To

LILA M ARGUE

few more souvenirs. Arriving in Nashville about 7 a.m., I freshened up at the Air National Guard facility on the airport grounds. In the locker room I saw an air technician friend of mine named Joe Williams. He asked me what I was doing there so early. My only reply was that I had just gotten back into town on an early flight and was preparing to go to the office.

He said, "I'm not going to be real chipper today. I stayed up late watching the Closing Ceremony at the Olympics on TV. It must have been after one before I got to bed."

I replied, "I missed a little sleep myself."

He still doesn't know.

Calgary — 1988

With big dollars and huge ticket volume, the Olympics attract world class con artists, some very sophisticated, as I discovered when ordering tickets to the 1988 Olympics in Calgary. Even though I had added my name to the mailing list for ticket applications in person at the headquarters of the Olympics Committee in Calgary, I came extremely close to losing not only my order for tickets, but my money as well — over $2,000.

I had followed the ordering instructions to the letter and mailed my cashier's check off to Canada. Months passed with no confirmation, nor any tickets. Sometime in the late summer or early fall of 1987, I received word that my application and check were found as part of a complex scheme to dupe ticket buyers. The Royal Canadian Mounted Police had become involved, and they recovered some applications from this bogus group.

When it was all over, I not only had every ticket I requested, but choice locations: forty-yard-line seats for the Opening and Closing Ceremonies; figure skating in the lower level behind Peter Jennings and his children, and more hockey game tickets than I had people to attend. Whether those choice seats were to compensate me for the fraud scheme, or were because I had registered in person, or were sheer luck, the Ticket Fairy worked her magic once more.

As Ginger and I had arrived a few days ahead of Sally and Morna, I had extra tickets to a preliminary hockey game, not one in great demand. One of my other diversions was Olympic pin collecting, something that I was introduced to at the Summer Games at Los Angeles in 1984. The madness had grown dramatically in the interim four years. There was a designated location in Calgary for pin swapping. Usually there was a gathering outside the venues dealing in this popular sideline. On this particular day outside the Saddledome I told Ginger to sell the two extra tickets for whatever she could get, while I went to check out the Olympic pins. Ginger was standing on the steps to the entrance to Saddledome, and I was at the bottom of

the steps. When I paused from the pin trading to check on Ginger, all I could see was the red light glowing on the ABC-TV camera and Ginger prattling away into the mike. Her reply was in the air. "Yes, I am from Nashville, Tennessee, and I am enjoying Calgary and the games. My husband wanted me to sell these tickets while he bought some Olympic pins." I was later told by a co-worker in Nashville that she heard Ginger's voice on TV and leaped from the bathtub and ran to see her on ABC at the Olympics.

What followed was somewhat embarrassing and totally unexpected. The cameraman and reporter were following us through the turnstiles with the red light aglow and down the steps to our seats at

center rink. With these great seats and the TV camera crew following us until we were comfortably seated, I became aware of the buzz going on around us, with comments like, "Who are they? They must be famous. Do you recognize them? Find out who they are." I felt as if we were under a microscope for the balance of the game. However, no one ever approached us with the obvious question. I did not bother to proffer to my seat mates that I was an inconsequential attendee at The Games, nor did I imagine that it would make for another unexpected experience along the trail to completing my Top 25 Major Sporting Events.

Ginger has always been full of surprises. Neither she nor the Ticket Fairy disappointed me at the Winter Olympics! I could have never have imagined this trip in 1986, much less make the plans for it.

My suggestion is to pursue the event, be flexible and let things flow. Do not sit and wait for it to happen or try to plan every detail to the nth degree. It may be easier on you mentally and save your heart to watch the Olympics or any other sporting event from the couch, but unknowns over the hill and the surprise around the corner will be missed. Life is wonderful!

The 1992 Winter Games in Albertville, France, would be a tough ticket, and I began my work early. All the ingredients of a ticket scarcity were present: Winter Games, where the Europeans excel, were being held in the heart of Europe; a small, remote village would be the host community; it was the last time the Winter and Summer Games would be held in the same year. This was another of those rare times when a personal connection, rather than persistence, could be the key to success. Mr. Joe M. Rodgers, the U. S. Ambassador to France, was a Nashvillian, and the friend of a friend. I forwarded a letter asking to be added to the mailing list for all the pre-event literature and a ticket application. These materials were mailed later in the year under the signature of one of France's greatest sports heroes, Jean-Claude Killey. The pride of France at hosting the Games was evident in the giant size of the brochures.

You're never more than two people away from almost any ticket you want. Ask friends and acquaintances whom they know who could help you.

In spite of my interest in the Games, I ended up not ordering any tickets in '92. But I tell the story to illustrate that you're always only two persons away from securing any ticket. You ask someone who knows someone else who can make it happen. Simple networking can be your ticket to adventure. My approach is to work backwards from the event. In the case of Albertville, I thought, "Who do I know in France?" The Ambassador was a Nashvillian. Who did I know who knew the Ambassador? My friend Buzz was a personal friend of the Ambassador. Thus, the link to the ticket source was complete.

You can apply this technique to any event, anywhere. (Ambassadors not required.) Start by letting as many people who may have a contact know what you're looking for. You'll be amazed at the insights people have in suggesting someone or someplace to check out. In turn, people will ask you for assistance from time to time in getting a scarce ducat, and you help them. It's like a blood bank. You give when it is easy, convenient, and helpful to those in need. Then your day comes when you need to go to the bank for an infusion of tickets. A side benefit is the chance to renew acquaintances and keep the lines of communication open.

Each year I contact friends and acquaintances, and meet new people, who may want to attend a Redskins home game, and my offer of two or four tickets is always welcomed. Even if they can't go, prospective guests appreciate being considered and sought out.

Our society has become a world of takers rather than givers. Buck the trend: Try offering someone you know a ticket or two. Proffering a gift with no thought of receiving anything beyond the ticket's face value in return will make someone's day, especially if a youth benefits.

Olympic Games — 1996

The greatest show on earth

The XXVI Olympiad in Atlanta was not only "Higher, faster, stronger," as the Olympic motto says, but also "Bigger." True to its billing, it was the most gigantic extravaganza in the history of sports, with more participating nations (197), more competing athletes (10,548), the largest budget ($1.6 billion), and more competitions (over 540).

In the South, the Centennial Games represented the most anticipated two weeks in history. By the Spring 1995, the Official Ticket Request Forms were already available at local Kroger stores and going fast. I ordered tickets for only nine events: Opening and Closing Ceremonies, a gymnastics session, one swimming competition, two track and field events, and three basketball sessions: two men's and one women's. According to the order form, those events would set me back $4,132.86, including Opening and Closing Ceremonies at $636 each, and men's basketball finals — where I expected to see the American Dream Team — at $265 per.

In October my confirmation order arrived. The ticket lottery had awarded me only three events, gymnastics, track and field, and women's basketball, and a credit balance of $3,542. A friend I had advised on ordering tickets, General J.R. Roberts, told me *he* had secured a pair of Opening Ceremony tickets! I told him I'd buy his second ticket if his wife Cardi decided she would rather go to Lennox Square instead. I still had plenty of time to find a ticket, though; no reason to get anxious!

In April 1996, my editor, John Perry, offered to accept Olympic tickets for his family of four in exchange for services rendered. Good idea! Dad takes children to the world's greatest sporting competition. John had already received tickets to soccer in Birmingham, and a preliminary round of women's basketball in Atlanta, and was hopeful of scrounging up tickets to another event or two. A May telephone call to the Olympic Ticket number in Atlanta proved very worthwhile. The most courteous and helpful person on the other end of the line advised me that previously sold-out events like gymnastics and basketball would be available on a first-come, first-served basis beginning at 9 a.m. EDT the next day. At 7:45 CDT that next morning, a Saturday, I started exercising my re-dial button, and continued to do so for two hours and thirty-five minutes! When I did talk to someone, I was in no rush to learn what tickets were available. There were $212 seats left for the gymnastics gold medal round. I knew the grandchildren would understand the event, as both were enrolled in gymnastics class in Salt Lake City. They couldn't care less about the cost. "Let me have four." My wife gagged from the kitchen when she heard that request. (She eavesdrops on my telephone conversations that involve money.) Gold medal men's basketball was also available at $265 per ticket —outrageous, but the urge was too strong to resist. Maybe I'd get the tickets I had originally wished for after all.

The combination of my tenacity and credit balance tipped somebody off to the fact that I was a serious Olympics fan. In mid-May I received a Special Invitation to Purchase Olympic Opening Ceremony Tickets. It proudly proclaimed, "Construction broadcast and technological requirements have been completed. These final configurations for various Olympic venues have allowed us to go on sale recently to the general public with new tickets to previously over-subscribed sessions." I ordered the maximum allowable of two $636 tickets on the spot. This checked off the last box on my wish list.

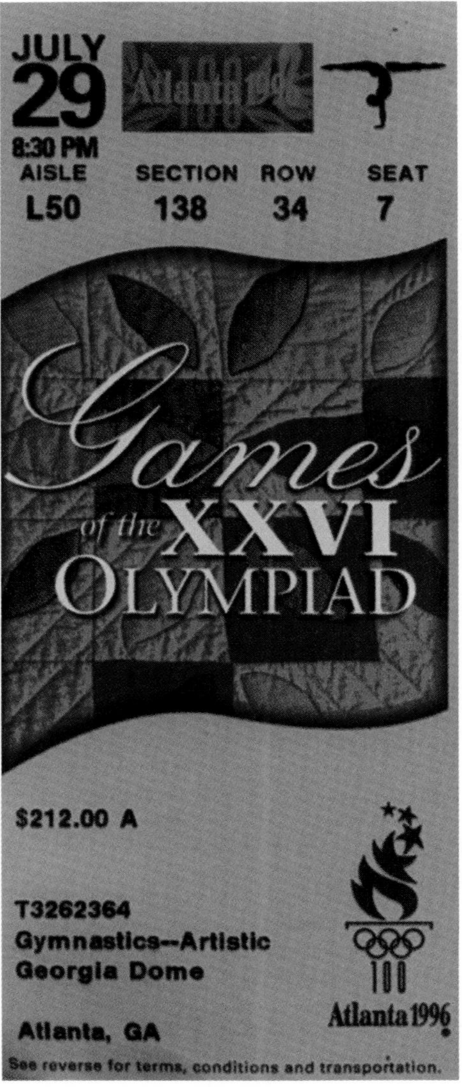

Arriving early outside the Olympic Stadium for the Opening Ceremony, Ginger and I mingled with the crowd, taking pictures, watching for people we might recognize, frequently sipping from my water container (it was hot) and walking under the cool-mist-spray structure thoughtfully erected for fans to cool off a bit. We went inside and were enjoying the food from one of the concessions when Donald Trump, his wife, and infant daughter entered. The mother and daughter walked off for a moment, leaving Mr. Trump standing there with his security detail and talking with a person in the crowd. I finished my hot dog and walked over to speak. I told him that I had enjoyed his book *The Art of the Deal.* He was very approachable and very gracious during our brief exchange. Ginger snapped a photo while Mr. Trump and I were standing together, but that picture and all the rest of my Opening Ceremony pictures were for naught as my recently repaired Nikon camera turned out not to have been repaired after all. I was both upset and disappointed. When I discovered the problem later at my seat, I asked a nice couple from Grand Rapids, Michigan, if they would provide me with a second copy of their Opening Ceremony prints. I hoped the camera of Richard and Mary Lou

Hoak worked better than mine.

Across the aisle from me at the Opening Ceremony sat pro golfer John Cook and his son. On a trip to get some water I commented to him, "John, you are at the wrong venue this weekend, aren't you?" The British Open was being played during this same period. To which he quickly replied, "No, not at all." I thought about that for a moment and agreed. He and his son were building a memory and enjoying a father/son experience that was a thrill for the boy and a once-in-a-lifetime treat for a PGA golfer. John Cook had his priorities straight. What I wish I'd said was, "John, I am glad to see you bypassed a trip to 'The Open' to go to the Olympics with your boy." First-time authors miss these openings for a quotable quote. I apologize to John Cook for asking the wrong question.

Seeing the Games

brought the same feelings as my three previous Olympics — patriotism, appreciation of the effort of the competition, and the enormity of the spectacle. Some sports journalists reported a side of the Games that I never personally experienced. I made three separate trips to Atlanta during the seventeen days of the Games, riding MARTA trains and/or buses from outlying areas to the Georgia Dome or Olympic Stadium. The crowds and waits that made such news were no worse than for a routine football weekend in the SEC, perhaps actually a little better.

As with all successful sporting events, the volunteers made the difference. For these Games the forty-five-thousand volunteers were always helpful, courteous, and usually well informed, though one notable exception proved amusing.

Returning from the men's and women's gymnastics gold medal rounds, I stood in line with my daughter and granddaughter for the bus back to the parking lot at Kennesaw College. After waiting in line for thirty minutes, we climbed aboard for what should have been a thirty-minute bus ride. When we came to the first traffic light after pulling away from the Georgia Dome, the bus driver turned around and asked, "Does anyone know how to get on I-75 North?" This poor volunteer from Memphis had no clue as to the exit route. After touring south Atlanta, going the wrong way on a one-way street (a dump truck stopped to let us by, thank goodness), someone in the front of the bus pulled out a city map and directed us to I-75. I was a little surprised to find no Atlantans knew the city streets. We finally made it back to the Fairfield Inn by 2 a.m. with two exhausted but exhilarated girls. Mother and daughter had tasted the Olympic adventure.

Lance, my grandson, had arrived at our house in Nashville on Saturday, July 27, with his mother and sister for the four of us to sample the Olympics on Monday. By Sunday he was breaking out with chicken pox. I didn't think his going would be any more dangerous than having some crazy bomber on the loose in Olympic Park. But his mother and grandmother out-voted me. Now I owe him one. Maybe a trip to Sydney when he is almost eight would be more memorable and meaningful anyway. Something to think about and plan for. And a great way to begin a sequel to *The Ticket* for the next millennium.

The world owes a Frenchman, Baron Pierre De Coubertin, a debt of gratitude for reviving the Olympics in Athens in 1896. His proposal to a gathering of the world's leading sports authorities on June 23, 1894, in the Grand Hall of the

Sorbonne in Paris, inspired the renewal of the Olympics. "I believe in the moral and peaceful virtues of sport," he said. "On the playing fields men are no longer political or social friends or enemies, but only fellow players, playing the same game."

His words were timely in the nineteenth century, but they face an uncertain future with the incredible changes in the U.S. culture of the 1990s. Amateur and emerging sports still hold to Coubertin's ideals, but I wonder if our established professional sports have lost their ability to reflect these truths. Do sports reflect a civilization's evolution — birth, infancy, maturity, and then an inevitable fade?

Please remember that each venue and each local government has ordinances regulating the resale of tickets. It's important to check out the laws and traditions in a community before you buy or sell a ticket. You could be breaking the law, and you run the chance of being fined and/or having your hard-won tickets confiscated.

Sometimes, brokers will create a "private association" to stay on the right side of the law. For a nominal membership fee, you may gain access to a private, closed setting where the broker buys and sells. My single experience with this type of marketplace was in a meeting room in a popular, accessible hotel at the '84 Games in L.A.

Any venue with limited seating capacity, final championships, and popular events with USA teams participating will have a high demand. Conversely, large stadium events, outdoor events subject to high temperatures, and up-and-coming sporting events will have more tickets available and lower prices. Take the grandchildren to those.

Eleven Final Fours

Success smothers this spectator

It's generally agreed that the NCAA basketball finals, the Final Four, is one of the two toughest tickets in sports. My experience confirms that. Four big college teams play in the tournament every year, each with students, alumni, contributors, friends, family, and fans who all want to attend. Hordes of media people are there. And then you find the sports junkies like me, all jockeying for the twenty-thousand tickets or so available in the biggest basketball arenas. (Plans call for permanently moving the Final Four to the giant indoor stadiums, which will provide twice as many tickets in the future, but we'll lose the feel and energy of the game. It may not be the same.)

I've made it to eleven Final Fours over the years, each with its own unique drama and excitement.

1959 — Freedom Hall in Louisville, Kentucky

University of California — Cincinnati — Louisville — West Virginia

West Virginia	94	Louisville	79	Semifinals
California	64	Cincinnati	58	Semifinals
Cincinnati	98	Louisville	85	Consolation
California	71	West Virginia	70	Championship

All four finalists this year were Top Ten teams except Louisville, with a 16-10 record. Two of the all-time greats, Jerry West and Oscar Robertson, had led their teams to the Final Four.

With Louisville only a little over two hundred miles away, four young avid basketball fans had to see this championship. Tickets

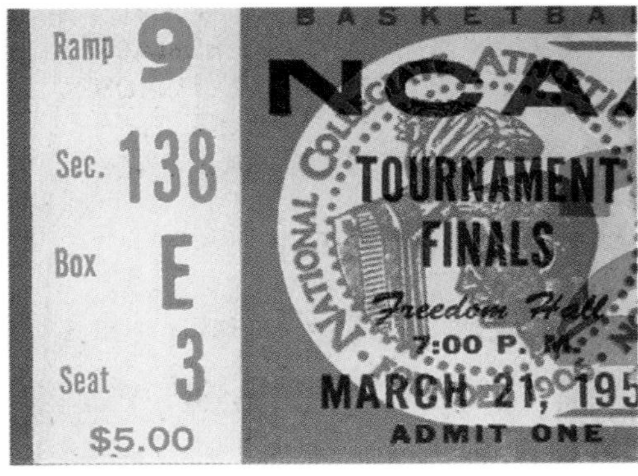

were difficult, but nothing like today, even with Louisville playing at home. One of our group, Jim Edwards, nailed down tickets through a former University of Louisville basketball player and fraternity brother, Dick Panther, that he knew for a couple of years. We stayed at the Louisville YMCA.

Coming up from Harriman in those pre-Interstate days, my route was U.S. 27 to 127, both basically two-lane highways. I was in Kentucky where the road was straight, wide, and carrying a minimum traffic on a Friday morning. My heavy foot naturally attracted the attention of a Kentucky trooper behind a rock wall cut through this hilly section for the roadbed. He not only pulled me over, but for some reason escorted me into the courthouse a few miles down the road. On the way to town, I noticed strings of posters along the road and in people's yards. The judge/magistrate I was to appear before was seeking re-election, and his face was all over town. I thought it only proper to show my support and, of course, seek his leniency on a little speeding charge. Without question I was going too fast. No point in trying an alibi. Before entering his chambers I located a campaign button for "His Honor" and wore it into his office. He looked at me, looked at the button on my jacket, and looked at the speeding ticket.

Without much ado, he said, "I appreciate your support for my re-election, young man. But as a Tennessee resident, you won't have a chance to vote for me. That will be $18.50 for speeding."

We resumed our trip to Freedom Hall to see speed in the proper context: the fast break of the Mountaineers, our team of choice since we had seen them in the Kentucky Invitational Tournament (KIT) in Lexington the two previous years. Three of the four of us had attended that tournament since its first year in 1953. Coach Rupp would invite the best in the country to his court for a Christmas season shoot-out. West Virginia was the first team to beat him in the KIT. We had watched these Mountaineers shoot pool in a downtown Lexington poolroom for hours on Saturday before they went on the floor that night to outrun the Wildcats. Not many teams did that in the '50s against Kentucky. So much for resting up ahead of the game.

Louisville had arrived for the Final Four after beating the now SEC champion, Kentucky, who had replaced the Mississippi State team. The Mississippi legislature had decreed coach Babe McCarthy's team would not play against Negroes. The Louisville team lost to West Virginia in the semis and the Big O was contained by the California man-to-man. This set up the finals between West Virginia and California.

California won at the buzzer with Darrell Imhoff shooting three times at the end and getting his own rebounds, ultimately scoring the winning basket.

"West Virginia was wonderful and Oscar was outstanding, but Darrell was the difference," California Coach Newell noted after the Golden Bears won, 71-70.

1960 — Cow Palace in San Francisco

University of California — Cincinnati — New York University — Ohio State

Ohio State	76	New York	54	Semifinals
California	77	Cincinnati	69	Semifinals
Cincinnati	95	New York	71	Consolation
Ohio State	75	California	55	Championship

I was living in Sacramento in 1960, which again put me within driving distance of my second consecutive Final Four. To get Final Four tickets that year, I just wrote and asked after arriving at Mather AFB in January, two months before the tournament. I traveled alone to the Cow Palace — not many basketball fans in my navigator-bombardier class.

On Friday night, during halftime of the Ohio State/NYU game, I entered the concession line behind a gentleman in a brown suit. When I recognized Coach Rupp, I was awestruck and elated. What should I say? Should I keep my mouth shut? I couldn't pass up a chance to speak to a basketball legend. Finally I said, "Coach, Ohio State looked mighty good in the first half!"

"Humh!" he barked. "They couldn't beat us during the season. We handled them." I later relayed that brief conversation to Jerry Lucas in 1988 and to Coach Jack Gardner in 1995.

Ohio State University won the championship after beating NYU 76-54, then rolling over the defending champions from California, 75-55. Besides Lucas, the Buckeyes had John Havilchek, Larry Siegfried, J. Roberts, and M. Nowell. Tonight Imhoff was held to eight total points and five rebounds.

Ohio State Coach Fred Taylor said, "Last year our boys couldn't have caught Marilyn Monroe in a phone booth. Now look at them. I used many of Pete's [Newell] ideas. And they paid off for us tonight."

1966 — Cole Field House at the University of Maryland

University of Duke — Kentucky — Texas Western — Utah

Kentucky	83	Duke	79	Semifinals
Texas Western	85	Utah	78	Semifinals
Duke	79	Utah	77	Consolation
Texas Western	72	Kentucky	65	Championship

This game is one of the most talked about in NCAA history. I've discussed it in detail elsewhere, but I will hit the high spots again here. My boss, Lieutenant Colonel Robert Stroop, got me two tickets to this tournament through his son, who was a member of the Maryland baseball team. As the host school for the tournament, the university's athletic department was allocated some tickets. The demand was nothing like it is today. In fact, I had my choice of seats.

In those days, when seats went right up almost to the edge of the court, I liked to sit under the basket. For this series we were on

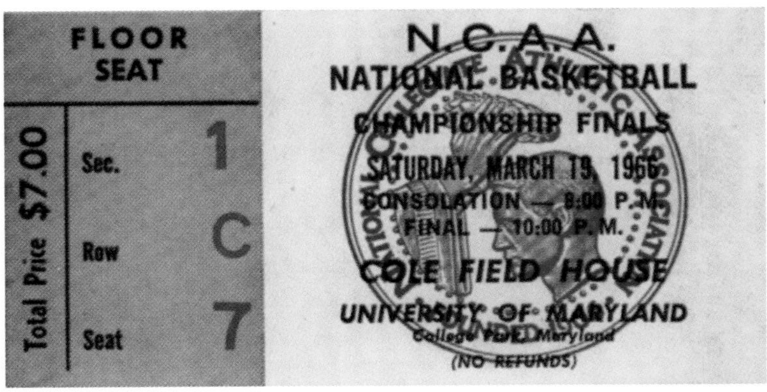

the third row behind the basket. You could feel the sweat splatter.

Ginger's roommate at the time, a Piedmont flight attendant, dated Bob Verga, the Duke All-American guard. Since we had been to Cameron Indoor Stadium, seating 9,314, during the Blizzard of '66 to see Duke play NC State, the women were for Duke. I was for Kentucky, the SEC representative.

The best game of the three was the Duke/Kentucky match-up, which the 'Cats won 83-79. Verga had a cold or the flu and scored only four points, two-of-seven from the field — not exactly an All-American's night. Texas Western defeated Coach Jack Gardner's Utah team 85-78. Until then, Coach Gardner was the only person to take two different teams twice each to the Final Four. Kentucky bested his Kansas State team in 1951 by a score of 68-58. As Coach Gardner was to tell me thirty years later, that 1951 loss was the hardest of his career, especially since he led 29-27 at halftime of the final game.

Coach Haskins used a 1-3-1 zone against Rupp's Runts that night and it neutralized the quick 'Cats. Many times during the regular season Kentucky would commit single-digit turnovers, as few as six. This night they were guilty of turning the ball over eighteen times, ultimately losing 72-65. Coach Rupp retired six years later without going past the second round. In fact, 1966 was the last time a segregated team was a serious challenge for an NCAA title. Rupp did integrate his team before he retired.

1982 — Superdome in New Orleans

Georgetown — Houston — Louisville — North Carolina

Georgetown	50	Louisville	46	Semifinals
North Carolina	68	Houston	63	Semifinals
North Carolina	63	Georgetown	62	Championship

This was my first Final Four in 16 years. UCLA's dominance, 1967 through 1973, had made the competition somewhat predictable and caused me to lose some interest. The Final Four in Atlanta in 1977 had looked promising, but the demand on my time and switching from a Friday-Saturday format to a Saturday-Monday night game created some scheduling problems.

In '82 when a friend at work, Larry Barnes, mentioned that a friend of his needed to sell his tickets, my interest in the Final Four began to stir again. He also needed to sell his prepaid room reservations at the Maison de Ville in New Orleans. An upcoming marriage had put him in a financial dilemma.

I got to the Superdome only to discover that the seats for Saturday's games were in the rafters. It was my first time to see basketball in a domed stadium, and the players looked like little bugs down there. I thought, "This stinks!"

Monday at lunch, I had a stroke of luck at Pascal's Manale restaurant in the Garden district, a big sports hang-out and fun place. Standing at the oyster bar, I realized the oyster lover standing next to me was Cliff Hagen, the Kentucky athletic director, a former All American and a hero of mine from Kentucky's undefeated 1953-54

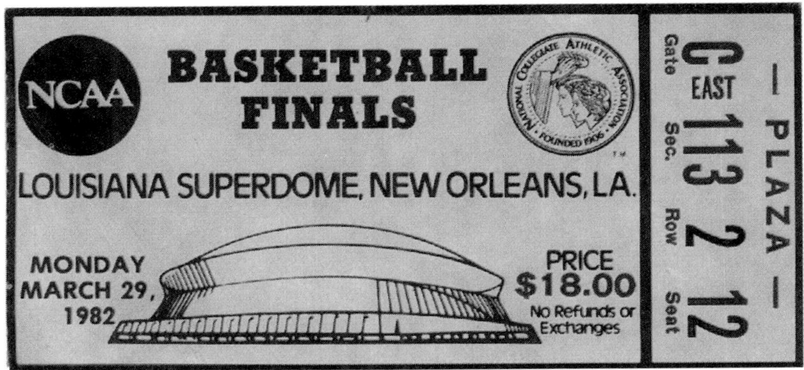

team. After a year's suspension they went 25-0, only for Rupp to decline an invitation to the NCAA tournament. His fifth-year seniors were ineligible to play.

Hagen was listed at six-foot-five and played center, but probably more significant, his handspan was purported to be fifteen inches — no doubt that partly explained his classic soft wheelhouse hook shot. There has never been one smoother, or more picturesque. I told my wife, "I think Cliff Hagen must have shrunk in the past thirty years, as he cannot be more than six-two or six-three."

Also at the bar were some young guys, probably students from one of the participating schools, bragging about having good seats for sale. I bought two on the second row behind the North Carolina bench. Anything to get out of the nose-bleed section.

James Worthy's steal of Sleepy Floyd's errant pass in the closing seconds is a classic moment for Final Four followers. It was right in front of us; we looked into Worthy's eyes. Michael Jordan's performance that night was prologue to his greatness. My image of the outcome of that game is Coach John Thompson's gracious congratulations to his friend, Coach Dean Smith. Coach Thompson's huge stature grew even greater in my eyes when he hugged the diminutive Dean Smith. While fans and players were going wild, old friends could share the moment and appreciate each other's feelings.

1984 — Kingdome in Seattle

Georgetown — Kentucky — Houston — Virginia

Georgetown	53	Kentucky	40	Semifinals
Houston	49	Virginia	47	Semifinals
Georgetown	84	Houston	75	Championship

Friends in Cocoa Beach, Florida, somehow rounded up four tickets for the Kingdome Final Four, providing an excuse for a trip larger than just a basketball play-off. The four of us had traveled together often to fun places including Rome, Capri, and Venice. Once our wives knew we were going, their comment was, "Oh, goodie. How long can we stay?"

After meeting at the Seattle-Tacoma airport, we were off to Port Townsend where the movie *An Officer and a Gentleman* was shot. Salmon fishing in Puget Sound with a photographer relative of Sally Ballew's made for an idyllic day. Fresh-caught salmon with chives and a bit of mayonnaise, the beautiful view, and the bracing wind are still fond memories. We took tea at the Princess Hotel in Victoria, described as the most beautiful city in North America. Then on to Bouchard Gardens, and finally to a ferry for the ride to Vancouver. A leisurely drive back through the vineyards and wineries of Washington state completed the loop that began in Seattle three days earlier.

We also had our share of situations that are contrary to my culture. An Air National Guard buddy recommended a hostel-type inn just off the University of Washington campus. When we arrived, the two women in charge gave us a copy of the house rules. No

showers after 10 p.m., no radios, no comings and goings after some hour, breakfast served between 8 a.m. and 9 a.m. OK, when in Rome!

Next morning I was up and about to find a newspaper, and smelled the aroma of bacon and eggs cooking in the kitchen. I could hardly wait to sample the offerings. Were we surprised! We sat down to one muffin, juice, and coffee or tea. The more elaborate freshly cooked meal was just for the two proprietors. Enough! We're out of there! The downtown Hilton was not so picturesque, but had no evening curfew.

Our seats in the Kingdome were high in the upper deck for the semis. But on Monday night before the game we walked from C.X. McCrory's tavern across from the Kingdome through the parking lot. I approached an athletic-looking couple getting out of their their luxury auto — I think the man was a former UCLA All American — and found that they had two extra tickets. I bought them on the spot.

Inside, Ginger and I found ourselves in section 101 next to Tom Hammond, who, at that time, broadcast SEC basketball games for Jefferson Pilot. My nose-bleed section tickets went begging. I sat watching the Final Four with the extra nose-bleed tickets in my pocket!

That night Guy Lewis's team was the bridesmaid for the second year in a row. The Phi Slamma Jamma heroes would have to wait until 1995 to taste the sweetness of a championship. Hakeem Olajuwon was reunited that year with his 1984 teammate, Clyde "The Glide" Drexler, and won it all in the NBA championship.

Coach John Thompson's team came back from the loss in New Orleans to win it all that night. True champions keep coming back until they win the prize.

1985 — Rupp Arena in Lexington

Georgetown — St. Johns — Villanova — Memphis

Georgetown	77	St. Johns	59	Semifinals
Villanova	52	Memphis	45	Semifinals
Villanova	86	Georgetown	64	Championship

One way to let people know you're in the market for tickets is to put up a sign. Not fancy, but effective. Ginger is barely five feet tall, but she can hold a sign above her head and garner plenty of attention. On our drive into Lexington Friday night, I wrote a message on the cardboard backing of a tablet I fished out of my briefcase. "Will Trade Redskins Tickets for Final Four Tickets." It produced results! The holder may have had more to do with that than the sign.

We found a motel room on the west side of town, when there were supposed to be no rooms available anywhere near Lexington. Our first stops on the ticket chase were the hotel lobbies of the NCAA headquarters and the team hotels. The Hyatt lobby was packed; no tickets available. We did meet a young ticket hustler from Dallas with whom I would later share a taxi from the airport at the NBA Finals in Houston in 1986.

The next morning we were at the Continental Hotel, the Hoyas headquarters. Ginger's sign brought an inquiry from a priest. He asked about three Redskins tickets. A Georgetown priest would obviously need to support his hometown team. After he went into the coffee shop to eat, my wife asked the registration clerk, "Do you know the name of the priest that I was talking to?" "Oh, yes," she said. "Father George! Isn't he beautiful?"

When he returned from breakfast, Father George invited us to his room to discuss a Redskins–for–Final-Four swap. He was looking for tickets for his parents who were in the room across the hall. We walked over to their room, Father George introduced us, and we visited awhile. Then Father George laid two books of Final Four tickets on the bed. This was late March and I wouldn't have my Redskins season tickets until July. I said, "Father George, you'll have to trust me on getting the tickets to you in the fall, when your parents decide which game they want to attend." To which he replied, "Jack, that is the business I'm in."

That meeting began a cordial relationship that lasted for several years. I would sell him 'Skins tickets for a game or two at the beginning of each season. Some years later I learned that a congressman had used the tickets that I had made available to Father George.

The sharing of scarce ducats knows no bounds.

1986 — Reunion Arena in Dallas

Louisville — Kansas — Duke — Louisiana State

Louisville	88	LSU	77	Semifinals
Duke	71	Kansas	67	Semifinals
Louisville	72	Duke	69	Championship

Earl and Eva Grace Ladd, lifelong friends of mine, lived in Dallas and knew enough of my avid enthusiasm for sporting events to invite us for a visit over Easter weekend — the time of the Final Four. Their invitation came midway through the basketball season and gave us time to make plane reservations for a crowded holiday travel time.

The Big East powers were absent that year, and the tourney had a more southern flavor. I could pull for any one of these teams — an SEC representative or Duke, which was re-entering the Final Four scene. Louisville was there, and I had always liked Denny Crum's

teams. He seemed to know how to get his team to peak at tournament time. How many times had he had ten losses, yet advanced in the NCAA Tournament? Of course, Kansas is the birthplace of college basketball, having spawned at least two legends, Coach Rupp and Dean Smith. The '86 Final Four had a lot of appeal for me.

Louisville and Duke survived the semis. Ginger and I sat behind the basket for these games, as our friend Earl had no interest in going to the session. Leaving the Arena, we saw a young couple wearing LSU colors with two tickets for the Monday night game. Their seats were an improvement over ours, so I bought them and later sold my original two.

For the Monday finals, I followed my dress-for-excitement rule: a bright purple and mauve Madras sport coat, white slacks, a pink shirt and a purple tie with light specks in it. As it turned out, I was glad I dressed up for the occasion. On the way into Reunion Arena, a group of young men were walking toward us, and obviously had had a beer or so. One looked at me and in the spirit of the moment said, "Hey man, where's your extension cord?" That comment summed up the effect pretty well and has been cited repeatedly when I've donned that ensemble since.

At any major championship, be alert to the frauds who may peddle counterfeit credentials. Professional ticket brokers know their business and the market. They will drive a hard bargain for great seats. The amateurs are obviously just trying to turn a fast dollar. If a deal appears too good to be true, the tickets in question are probably counterfeit or stolen.

We were seated at center court about eighteen or twenty rows back and got plenty of stares. I assumed my outfit was continuing to attract its due amount of attention. Eventually a policeman arrived with an older couple. They asked us to leave. We were in the middle of the NCAA official party. Our tickets belonged to the couple and had been stolen! The young couple I had bought them from had lifted them from the NCAA official's pocket!

We were escorted to the back of the arena. The police officer was very understanding. He said, "The tickets were reported stolen and had it been someone besides an NCAA official representative, who would have known? Ordinarily, lost or stolen tickets are without any recourse."

We nervously awaited his ruling. My outfit must have persuaded him that I was not a thief, just a dumb gullible fan. When I explained the circumstances he allowed us to stay in the arena, as long as we didn't obstruct anyone's view or block the passageways. I went to the front row where the press was seated — some had observed my ouster. One vacant seat was available next to Gus Manning, an associate athletic director from UT. I sat down and asked who had the seat. He said, "So-and-so from a KC newspaper, but he's not returning for the finals." I stayed put. Ginger, I thought, is usually good at fending for herself.

The moral of the story is two-fold: dressing for a sporting event may help you more than you can imagine later. Secondly, beware of ticket sellers if their prices appear too good to be true.

1988 — Kemper Arena in Kansas City

Oklahoma — Arizona — Kansas — Duke

Oklahoma	86	Arizona	78	Semifinals
Kansas	66	Duke	59	Semifinals
Kansas	83	Oklahoma	79	Championship

I invited two young cousins and a local young accounting buddy for a guys' trip to Kansas City. I spent the time outside the arena trying to keep up with three young guys in their twenties. They were determined to see all of Kansas City. I wanted to be able to report to their wives that we did at least a few things of cultural or historical significance.

Saturday, we sat in the second level at the top of the key behind the proud parents of Quinn Snyder, a Duke guard, who were gracious in defeat.

On Sunday we toured Harry S. Truman's home in Independence, Missouri, and the first mall in the U.S. at Mission City, Kansas. We also scoped out prospects for attending the Opening Day of baseball for the KC Royals on Monday afternoon. The game was a sell-out except for 5,000 tickets that would go on sale Monday at the stadium box office.

The chase was on!

Even with our early arrival at the stadium on a crisp, beautifully clear day, the ticket windows already had long lines. We found a stand-alone booth on the backside of the Royal's stadium with a line shorter than the others. I told the guys to get in line and I would be back. I approached a teenager near the front of the line and asked, "How many tickets are you buying?" Whatever the number was, he was four under the maximum. I had no idea how long the ticket supply would last with the long lines formed at ticket windows all around the stadium. I gave him a large bill and asked, "Would you buy me four and keep the change?' He was elated at the prospect of keeping the change on three dollar tickets thanks to his position in line. When he gave me my four tickets, I went to the end of the line to get my buddies. "Let's go. I've got us seats."

We were down the left field line on the second or third row. Since we were early for the game, I walked around to the Royals' dugout on the first base side to see if I could speak with a rookie named Scotty Madison. He had played at Vanderbilt and had been a recent guest of Buzz Davis's at Augusta National. Buzz had asked me to send his greetings if I got the chance. Scotty came over during an idle moment, and I passed the message along. He in turn wanted me to tell Buzz that he had an autographed baseball bat for him.

Back in my seat, I saw that Jerry Lucas was sitting across the aisle from me. I wanted to speak to him about a book of his that I had bought some time in the '70s. He had done an analysis of numbers and sequences of the Bible to arrive at various calculations and had put his conclusions in a book called *Theomatics: God's Best Kept Secret Revealed.* I walked over to him and said that I had seen him play the Final Four at the Cow Palace in 1960 when they won it all. Then I relayed the conversation I had had with Coach Rupp in the concession line. He reaffirmed the accuracy of Coach Rupp's comments.

I then ventured into deeper waters when I said, "I've read your book." Somewhat tersely, yet diplomatically he queried, "Which one? I've written twenty-two," or some such number. I looked for a hole to crawl in.

Six years later I spoke to him again at Judson Baptist Church in Nashville, where he was speaking on his memory-aid books. (His memory skills are phenomenal.) After twenty years, I bought my second book written by Jerry Lucas. Neither has anything to do with basketball or sports!

What a time line: the Final Four in 1960; his book on numbers in the Bible in the '70s; sitting next to him at a baseball game during the '88 Final Four; later, in 1994, hearing him speak and buying his book on U.S. Presidents. Maybe Jerry will read this book and add another piece to the puzzle.

1993 — Superdome in New Orleans

North Carolina — Kansas — Michigan — Kentucky

North Carolina	78	Kansas	68	Semifinals
Michigan	81	Kentucky	78	Semifinals
North Carolina	77	Michigan	71	Championship

My wife was going to Salt Lake City for two weeks, so she was off the traveling team for the '93 Final Four in New Orleans. With two tickets in hand, I called my friend Jack Burch to see if he wanted to go. He was reluctant at first, but his son John encouraged him. I warned him that all I had were tickets. No rooms, no flight reservations. He was game for it, so off we went.

Burch's resourcefulness produced a room at the Hyatt next to the Superdome for Saturday, Sunday, and Monday nights. These rooms turned out to be the non-bedroom portions of a large suite that had been used for hosting parties during the week leading up to the tournament. A Murphy bed and a roll-away for me were just grand. As Jack is the Avis franchisee for most of Tennessee, transportation was a done deal.

Arriving early in the afternoon before the Saturday game, we walked into the wild revelry of the Hyatt lobby. Rawlings Sporting Goods had a huge basketball, two or three stories in diameter, suspended from the spacious atrium ceiling that has become a Hyatt trademark.

In the connecting mall between the hotel and the 'Dome, the NCAA had a great basketball historical display. A pictorial history of previous Final Four highlights was organized by decade along the walkway. As we studied each display, I was particularly interested in seeing the eight tournaments I had attended.

I stopped in my tracks and motioned for Burch when I saw a photograph from the April 1, 1991, *Sports Illustrated* of the losing Kentucky bench after the 1966 loss to Texas Western, now UTEP. A feature article on the twenty-fifth anniversary of that game was entitled, "The Night They Drove Old Dixie Down." One of the photographs on the NCAA display was used in that article. A much younger Ginger and I, with my boss Lieutenant Colonel Robert Stroop, were standing behind the Kentucky bench. Burch was speechless.

Going to the 'Dome for Saturday's semifinals, I waved to my Rawlings friend, Randy Roberts, who had brought a customer of his, Tony Bender, the buyer for Champs stores in Bradenton, Florida. Randy escorted him around that year and again in 1994 in Charlotte. He was a special customer who dealt in Rawlings and New Balance merchandise. Randy has the eight- or nine-state Southeast sales region for Rawlings, New Balance, Ray Ban, and a couple of other lines of high-quality sports merchandise. His company, Sports Distributors Inc. in Knoxville, has a strong reputation in Tennessee high school athletics, as well as at large retail outlet chains in the Southeast. He's been a good friend and a thoughtful provider of sample merchandise.

Sunday evening, Burch and I journeyed to the Garden district to refresh my fond memories at Pascal's Manele. No Cliff Hagen nor extra tickets being sold at reasonable prices this trip. But the raw oysters were as good as ever.

After the semifinals and two full days of sightseeing, eating, and the sea aquarium, the finals were somewhat anti-climactic after my team was eliminated. But I was enjoying my visit with Jack, pointing out all the popular athletes, coaches, and media people. It was a real Who's Who on parade for four or five days. You won't feel the aura of this crowd-watching from the comfort of your living room.

In the finals, the now infamous time-out called by Chris Weber of Michigan left no doubt as to the outcome. With eleven seconds remaining and Michigan trailing by two, a technical was assessed since Michigan had no time-outs left. I had now witnessed Coach Dean Smith win two NCAA titles, both here in the Superdome.

1994 — Charlotte Coliseum

Arkansas — Arizona — Duke — Florida

Arkansas	91	Arizona	82	Semifinals
Duke	70	Florida	65	Semifinals
Arkansas	76	Duke	72	Championship

For the second consecutive year the '94 Final Four was an easy drive from Nashville. But this year an invitation to the Coaches' Dinner on the Thursday evening before the tournament meant a lengthy trip, a week altogether for only two evenings of basketball.

My friend with Rawlings, Randy Roberts, invited Ginger and me to a most enjoyable evening. I had the opportunity to meet some new people and hear Charles Kuralt interview the four coaches in the tournament. Seeing the SEC Commissioner Roy Kramer revived a memory of a lost dream.

In 1989, Coach Kramer had accepted the position of Commissioner, leaving his post as athletic director at Vanderbilt. He had spoken of some changes that he envisioned for the SEC, expanding the conference membership, a championship game for the conference title after establishing a two-division conference, and the possibility of relocating conference headquarters. Moving the headquarters was interesting to me, especially if he restructured the commissioner's office.

Eventually I got the chance to interview for a position under Coach Kramer. We exchanged possibilities of a role for me over the next several months. His vision was expansive and far reaching, and it would have been fun, as well as an honor, to have been on his team. Coach Kramer understood collegiate athletics, played within the rules, yet marketed the games for maximum conference and member-school revenue. But an offer was not forthcoming.

Back to 1994 and Randy Roberts's continuing generosity with an invitation to the corporate sponsor's pavilion near Charlotte Arena. The pre-game fetes there featured huge spreads with unique themes for each of the four festivities — pre- and post-game feeds, for both semis and finals. All this, and then a short walk to the Arena.

Two SEC teams were bracketed opposite each other in the semis. Duke was too much for Lon Kruger's Gators. In the Arizona/Arkansas game Nolan Richardson's "forty minutes of hell" defense won out, but it could not stop Lute Olsen's Wildcats firing from beyond the three-point arc for thirty-two three-pointers that night. Arkansas players never saw a three-point shot they didn't like. Between the two teams, a Final Four record was set with fifty-six three-pointers attempted.

Monday night, after leaving the spread at the hospitality pavilion, we noticed long lines forming to enter the arena. "What is going on?" asked Randy. Once in the queue, we learned that President Clinton's motorcade had halted the traffic en route to the coliseum. Now each fan had to pass through a security check prior to admission. The process took about an hour, and those who missed the tip-off could be most upset, if not hostile. The President sat in one of the enclosed center court boxes, and his longtime love for the Hogs was rewarded with their championship win.

Through the generosity of the Rawlings and New Balance Southeast regional representative, Ginger and I sampled a part of the Final Four that we never thought possible — the Coaches' Dinner and the Corporate Sponsors' fete, before and after both sessions.

1995 Seattle Kingdome

UCLA — Arkansas — Oklahoma State — North Carolina

UCLA	74	Oklahoma	61	Semifinals
Arkansas	75	N. Carolina	68	Semifinals
UCLA	89	Arkansas	78	Championship

This was Final Four number eleven and my second Final Four in Seattle. Must be getting close to the end when I start doing repeats. Part of the lure of sports is the adventure of going to a different locale and exploring all the area has to offer: Seattle is a great destination. Both the city and Puget Sound are gorgeous; mountains to the east and west are spectacular, and the walks along the waterfront and the restaurants have a nice feel. Everything is close by, yet you feel a spaciousness with the water so near.

One of the great joys of the trip was riding the ferry to Seattle from my quarters every day. The folks at Bangor submarine base on Bainbridge Island accommodated me for four nights. It was remote, but the Northwest beauty is something to behold.

Friday before the tournament I contacted Jim Kleinworth in Pasco, Washington. Jim and I had met through his brother-in-law, Jay Archer, at the Final Four in Dallas in 1986. Jay and his wife Jackie are friends in Nashville from Air National Guard days. Well, Jim goes to all the Super Bowls, we had made contact in San Diego in 1988, and he had used my Redskins tickets to watch the Seahawks at RFK. He chases sports about like I do. I asked him to join me for the tournament. He was delighted, and his home-course knowledge of Seattle would help us navigate around town. I warned him that the seats were in the third level, but at least we were in. Undeterred, he joined me.

Later on Friday, I went to see part of the practice sessions. At one of the entrances I noticed all the color-coded passes for the official party — coaches, press, NCAA officials, corporate sponsors, and so forth. Each had a unique color on the border of the seven-by-four-inch laminated card to be worn around the neck. I filed that information away, but not well enough.

Jim and I met at

his hotel on Saturday and started working our way through Pioneer Park to McCrory's restaurant across from the Kingdome. All the restaurants and bars in the area were a frenzy of activity. Jim wanted to stay at McCrory's longer than I did, so I went on alone to the Dome and watched the crowd, celebration, students, coaches, and others going to the game.

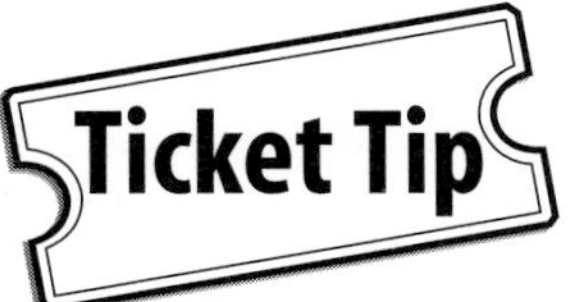

After the Final Four semifinals on Saturday, tickets for Monday's championship game break loose. Students from the teams that lose are ready to return home and usually want to make a few extra bucks. They will only be able to get the market price, but that will still be two to six times face value depending on location. Plus, by Monday night the festivities of the week wane, and I think some coaches, press, and corporate sponsors are ready to sell their tickets as well. Some are priced higher than the prudent buyer is willing to pay, but there is another source. Check the NCAA headquarters hotel for the action. More ticket reselling goes on at the Final Four than any single sporting event. Decide in advance what your upper limit will be. Don't get swept up in the excitement and pay more than it's worth to you.

Arkansas and UCLA prevailed in the semis, and now Arkansas had a chance to repeat! As an SEC fan, I liked those prospects.

Sunday at the Final Four is often Easter, but not this year. It was a beautiful but chilly day. I love the west coast seaside drives, so I took a loop around Olympic National Park. U.S. 101 starts at Olympia going north past Port Angeles along a scenic route west, and then south on the western edge of the national park, partly along a gorgeous seaside drive.

I caught up with Randy on Monday and visited the Coaches' Exhibition in the center adjacent to the Westin Hotel. I chatted briefly with an assistant coach at the University of Texas, Eddie Oran, who was from my hometown of Harriman, Tennessee.

For the finals, I had a real surprise in store. I decided to try trading up to better seats, and I bought a coaches pass from what turned out to be a master con artist at the headquarters hotel. The pass that I thought was legitimate gained me admittance to the CBS hospitality tent outside the 'Dome, but it was denied inside. It was a counterfeit! The security people were nice enough to allow me to remain in the stadium, but not in the inner sanctum where holders of genuine tickets could pass. I climbed back up to the third level to see Arkansas lose to a fired-up UCLA team.

Final Four tickets are prizes that grow steadily more impossible to come by. When I attended my first couple of tournaments, I ordered tickets by mail. Now demand has made getting them next to impossible. For a couple of Final Fours I had a private source, but it no longer exists. It's possible for you to get them — for a price — from brokers, buy them in town before the game, or enter the lottery.

The Masters — 1965, '66, '85, '86, '88, '89, '93, '96

Still the best

The toughest ticket in sports is the Masters. I say that in spite of having been there eight times. The irony of the situation is that tickets are quite reasonable.

Practice rounds on Monday or Tuesday are $16, climbing to $21 for Wednesday. A four-day tournament badge is a very nominal $100. But to keep the venue uncrowded for the benefit of players, members and their guests, the number of tickets is *strictly* limited.

Practice round tickets are no longer sold on a day-by-day basis at the gate. Applications have now been taken to compile a ticket holder database similar to the one for tournament badges that has been in existence for over thirty years, perhaps longer. I am on the practice-round list. In fact, you can no longer add your name to the waiting list for the four-day badge. My understanding is that the daily practice-round passes are awarded by lottery draw.

It's worth the price of admission to stroll Augusta National and then walk around the Par 3 course. On that course there are six water holes, four of which require shots across the ponds. The concluding event of the three days of practice brings out some of the legends. Arnold Palmer, Sam Snead, Doug Ford, Billy Casper, and Gary Player were just a few of the seventy-eight golfers participating in the 1996 event.

The Par 3 event is often overlooked. Some of the golfers view winning it as a hex. The winner of the Par 3 has never gone on to win the Masters in the same year. Eight former Masters champions have won the event, however: Sam Snead twice in 1960 (the first Par 3 contest) and 1974, but he lost three others in sudden death play-offs. Two former Masters champions, Art Wall, Jr. and Gary Brewer, hold the Par 3 record of 20. In the first thirty-six years of

this event there were twenty-nine holes-in-one. In the 1996 event there were four holes-in-one, one on #7 by Ian Baker-Finch. There is a story behind that one.

Late Tuesday afternoon, when all the golfers were off the eighteen-hole course and headed for their lodgings or the practice tee, Buzz Davis, Randy Roberts, and I were on the balcony of the Tennessee cottage overlooking #7 on the Par 3 course. A single golfer was on #7 tee hitting shots into the green. Buzz said, "Let's go down and speak to him after he finishes his practice shots."

We were at the back of the green when he walked up with his caddie. He had hit four shots into the green, all different shots to the pin that was situated back left. He had hit one straight at the flag, a fade, a draw, and a low run-up shot. One he holed for a birdie. He came to the edge of the green and spoke to Buzz, who introduced Randy and me. It was Ian Baker-Finch, who volunteered that when people asked him about his favorite golf course, "I tell them it is the Par 3 at Augusta." He seemed so genuine and such a very likeable chap from Australia. I accepted his unsolicited comment as gospel. He just likes to play that test of golf in an unrushed and uncrowded setting at day's end. After he gave each of us one of the Titleists that he hit into #7, we walked back to the Tennessee cottage.

The rest of the story unfolded less than twenty-four hours later during the Par 3 competition. Randy and I were on the balcony again

Wednesday with Lip and Kim Davis, Tom Baker, Tom Housewright, and Buzz's daughters, Adelaide and Gigi when Ian Baker-Finch stepped up to the #7 tee. A hole-in-one! Could not happen to a nicer guy.

Most years at the Masters, I spend the first day walking the entire course just to refresh my feel for this majestic nursery-turned-golf course. One of the privileges of being there in person is watching those holes on the front nine that the TV viewing audience never gets to see. I think that's just another way of saying to their loyal season ticket holders, "We appreciate you and your faithfulness to this spring event. Thank you for conducting yourself properly while you are our guests on this three-hundred-plus acres of beauty. We're saving half of the course for you alone." The club does that in other ways — very reasonable prices for admission and for the delicious fare at the concessions, free hand-outs of the pairings, and pamphlets for the benefit of the spectators. There is no classier event in sports than the Masters.

Much ado is made of Amen Corner, holes 11-12-13, with the old adage that the tournament begins on the back nine on Sunday. In other words, you don't win the Masters without playing Amen Corner successfully. But for my money, the toughest part of the course is a section that only the on-site spectators get to view: holes 3-4-5 and sometimes #6, depending on pin placement. In the 1996 Masters, Greg Norman played holes 3-4-5 in the first four rounds in two-over, and 11-12-13 in one-under; Faldo, the winner, played 3-4-5 in the first three rounds in two-over, and 11-12-13 in two-under. That is a very small sampling, but it shows those holes' effect on the two prime contenders for the championship.

At my first Masters in 1965, the cumulative tournament statistics for those six holes were:

Hole	Difficulty (1=most difficult)
3	11
4	1
5	4
11	5
12	2
13	17

In four other years that I have attended, the results of the Championship were as follows:

		3-4-5	11-12-13
1966 (tie)	Brewer	+4	-4
	Jacobs	+1	-1
	Nicklaus	-1	+2
1985	Langer	+1	-6
1986	Nicklaus	+3	-1
1988	Lyle	-2	+2

This debate will continue, and TV will continue to stress that the championship turns on the play at Amen Corner, but many will argue that it is holes 3, 4, and 5 where the tournament is won or lost. Strong evidence supports that premise. Those spectators in attendance can see it live and judge for themselves.

In my most recent Masters a couple of milestones occurred. Greg Norman tied the course record of 63. While I did not see that much of his round on the first day, I did follow the fellow who had previously held the low round of 63, Nick Price. He played the back nine in 30 on Saturday of the 1986 event. On holes 10 through 16 he played six under par. In Norman's record-tying 63, he birdied six of the last seven holes on the back nine. Earlier on that same day, Phil

Mickelson also shot a 30 on the back nine with birdies on 11-13-14-15-17 and 18. On Sunday, Faldo became the fourth three-time champion to put on the green jacket, joining Jimmy Demaret, Sam Snead, and Gary Player. Arnie won four times, and Jack Nicklaus is the all-time leader with six green jackets in his closet.

Of my eight Masters I've seen only four different winners, Jack Nicklaus, Nick Faldo, Bernhard Langer, and Sandy Lyle. Among the four they hold twelve Masters titles.

Of my eight Masters I've also had only four different ticket sources. For the 1965 trip, Bo Roberts had just gone to work for AT&T in Atlanta and invited me to join him for the four days. But he ended up not attending, as he was moving back to Knoxville and couldn't spare the time. At Augusta that year I ran into Jim Edwards and a group of his buddies with ALCOA, one of whom was from Augusta. We all stayed at the charming and aptly named Shady Oaks motel. Through that experience I was invited to join them for the 1966 Masters. There was a waiting list for badges that year, but it was nothing like the demand by the time I returned again in 1985.

The Davises rent a house for the week and invite couples in for a few days at a time. In 1985, Ginger and I were included for the Wednesday through Friday rounds. The next year, 1986, my YMCA buddy Neil Parrish secured badges for me for the Saturday and Sun-

day rounds. In the Sunday round we were standing by the bridge on #15 when Seve Ballesteros dumped his shot to a watery death and ended his hopes of a championship with a six on the Par 5. It was the only time I heard a rude Master's patron. There was applause for his misfortunes. Nicklaus made an eagle three, a swing of three shots. He held on to par 18 to beat Tom Kite by one stroke. Nicklaus shot a 72-hole total of 279, and Ballesteros went on to bogey 17 and finish at 281 — one of the great finishes of all time.

For my last four visits to the Masters I continue to be indebted to my mentor and friend Buzz Davis, who invited me back in 1988, 1989, 1993, and 1996. But here's the key question: If you don't have a friend like Buzz, how do you get your hands on the toughest ticket in sports?

I overheard a white-haired lady at this year's Masters who was in the company of Tom Kite, Sr. She remarked that her father used to have seventy-five Masters tickets. Now they have four. As she must have been in her seventies, her dad must have had that cache of tickets in the '40s or '50s. With more people having fewer tickets per household the prospects are reduced, but you may find season ticket holders who will let you use their badges for a day or two. But, should you be so fortunate, NEVER sell those to anyone lest your friends' worst nightmare come true — removal from the annual season ticket holder list.

In 1995 I was told by a ticket broker that a four-day badge would cost $3,500, and a one-day practice round would be $300. This year, 1996, I heard that two boys about thirteen or fourteen years old were offered $6,000 each for their badges. The prospective purchaser pursued them all the way to the gate with his offer. The boys stood firm and entered the Masters. A couple walking along watched the proceedings and asked the buyer if he was serious about buying two tickets. He was, and they had no such scruples as the boys before had shown. The buyer then peeled off one hundred Ben Franklins — $10,000 for two badges.

Counterfeiting is a real threat to some sporting events, but the Masters ticket office headed off that trend a few years ago by having an electronic code embedded in every badge. Only authentic badges will be passed by the card-reading equipment at each entrance.

I can't imagine what will happen in the future, as the supply remains constant and the demand increases exponentially. But you can be sure that as the price of bootlegged badges goes up, the scams will increase. Beware of your ticket source.

Winds of Change

College All-Star football game — 1953

Only a memory

Times and tastes change. Sometimes that means a once-great sporting event loses its popularity and fades from view. One event that change has robbed us of is the College All-Star football game. Arch Ward was the genius behind the first All-Star baseball game sponsored by the *Chicago Tribune* in 1933. The All-Star football game continued from 1934 to 1976, with the All-Stars winning only nine times.

To a sixteen-year-old sports fan, the prospects of seeing the football All-Stars in Chicago pumped me plenty. I ordered my tickets

directly from Soldier's Field, and during the summer days before this early August spectacle, I enlisted a buddy to go with me. Persuading his parents to let him take a seven-hundred-mile trip required the help of my parents. They assured Bill Staples' folks that, even though I had never been to Chicago, I could be trusted for the journey and could get around in that big city. Looking back on it today, their confidence in me was remarkable. I had no qualms about going on the Southern Railway to Cincinnati, then changing to the New York Central for Chicago. My dad and I had traveled by rail to Cincinnati for baseball games, sometimes continuing to Detroit to see the Tigers.

Luckily I reserved rooms at the Hilton Hotel, formerly the Stevens, where the Detroit Lions were staying for All-Star week. As the defending NFL champions, they would play the best of the 1952 college All-Stars, led by Coach Bobby Dodd of Georgia Tech. Sitting in the lobby and watching the Lions' players and their antics were eye-openers to a teenager from the hills of Tennessee. A defensive back, Jack Christiansen, would flirt with the seemingly endless stream of attractive blondes strolling through the lobby. Amazing how those images left an impression on me.

Bill and I arrived in time to hear Les Paul and Mary Ford at one of Chicago's theaters. We made a trip to Wrigley Field to see the Cubs. There was also a restaurant named La Boheme that featured wild game, as I recall. Lots of impressions for a sixteen year old.

Days before leaving, I had lost the ticket I was so proud of, or someone lifted it. I had the section, row, and seat numbers memorized. Frantically I had written to the ticket office at Soldier's Field. They responded with an admission pass showing my seat location.

Securing a replacement ticket today would be impossible.

Those days of believing, trusting people helping a young lad avert potential disaster are only a memory.

So is the College All-Star football game.

A side note: I had a chance to discuss this game with one of the Lions players forty-three years later. Jimmy "Cowboy" Hill was a Lions defensive back and Jack Christiansen's roommate. When I described Jack's antics in the Hilton Hotel lobby all those years ago, Jimmy noted, "That's Jack!"

He also passed along an interesting bit of sports trivia. Jimmy had played with the Lions in the '53 game I saw, and he had played on the College All-Star team in the 1951 contest after a great career at the University of Tennessee. He had been able to play in '53 only because he had two weeks of military leave, and his commanding officer had allowed him to rejoin the Lions for that summer spectacle.

I asked Jimmy how many players on that great Lions team had gone on to the Pro Football Hall of Fame. He quickly mentioned his former roommate Jack Christiansen, who had since passed away, Doak Walker, and Bobby Layne. I asked, "Didn't Leon Hart make it to the Hall of Fame?" "I don't think so," he replied. "Leon was too nice a guy, not mean enough for a pro career. He was so smart and could talk to anybody and make them feel comfortable and at ease. He was a giant of a person."

The Lions had all been big that night as they beat the College All-Stars 24-10.

Turning the Lights On at Wrigley Field —8/8/88

Illuminating the illustrious past

Wrigley Field, the museum and living legend of baseball, made history that night by succumbing at last to the unheard of — night baseball!

Most baseball fans know that the first major league night baseball game was played in 1935 at Crosley Field in Cincinnati. But in the Cubs research for the program this evening, Bill Deane documented several nuggets of trivia:

■ The first night baseball game was played 108 years earlier in 1880 at Nantucket Beach, Massachusetts. Lamps were propped on 300-foot towers surrounding a baseball field. Two amateur teams played to a 16-16 tie, concluding at 9:30 p.m. before 300 spectators.

■ The Tigers were the last A.L. team to host a night game in Briggs Stadium. Prince Hal Newhouser threw a two-hitter in a 4-1 win over the White Sox.

■ In the first night game at Brooklyn's Ebbets Field on June 15, 1938, Cincinnati's Johnny Vander Meer tossed his second consecutive no-hitter. Unmatched since.

■ This fabled evening may rank alongside or even outshine Game Three of the 1932 World Series in which Babe Ruth allegedly "called" his homerun shot off Cubs pitcher Charlie Root.

The hype and anticipation leading up to Wrigley's first night under the lights, August 8, 1988, was akin to the moon walk of astronaut Neil Armstrong twenty years earlier. *One and a half million people* called for tickets when the 12,756 that were available to the general public went on sale June 28. The Cubs would be turning on the lights more than five decades after the first night baseball game and almost four decades after the Detroit Tigers became the last to do so. Baseball tradition runs deep. It is part of the lure to the sport.

At a meeting I was attending at a north Chicago hotel, my host John Henry mentioned that over forty-million telephone call attempts had been made to the ticket office for the game. When I told Mr. Henry that I planned to try to get a ticket that evening outside Wrigley Field, he had only five words of advice. "Don't go near the place."

That was like waving a red flag in front of me. I recalled my and Ginger's success with a sign at the 1985 Final Four, and I made another one:

WILL TRADE TWO BEARS/REDSKINS TICKETS
FOR ONE TICKET TO THIS GAME

With a plan in hand, I drove off to Medinah Country Club to see the Monday play-off round for the U.S. Senior's Open championship. Gary Player and Bob Charles, the left-hander, would be in an eighteen-hole play-off for the title. I followed them for a few holes and was standing near the tee after they drove from a par-four. Player stopped for a cup of water, finished in a quick swallow, and handed me the cup with the request, "Would you please dispose of this for me?" I turned to look for the wastebasket near the water cooler when a host of women surrounded me, all squealing "Can I have that cup?" I was startled to find that a used water cup could be such a cherished memento. I handed it to the nearest Player fan and departed for my quest at Wrigley Field.

Walking around the main entrance at Wrigley before the game with my sign, I generated a fair amount of conversation with the baseball fans. "When is the game?" "Do you have any Bears/Packers tickets?" "Do you have the tickets with you?" Not only were the answers "No," but the game would be played at RFK Stadium in Washington. One family had some interest in the football tickets but did not have an extra ticket for that night's game. I had no interest in selling my tickets. I only wanted to swap for this history-making event on 8/8/88.

One fellow walked up to me and said, "You are offering too much for a ticket to this game. Come with me." I followed him to the will-call window where he picked up his envelope. He turned with a single ticket for me. "How much do you want for it?" When he replied, "Just the face value," I uttered an astonished prayer of thanks.

The evening's pre-game festivities, ending with the "Turning the Lights On" ceremony, was one of those times you knew was an historic moment. The game moved along and the storm moved in. A downpour wiped out the game before the official game of five innings was completed. Seeing the wind at near gale forces, and the fans beginning their mass exodus for cover, I knew that this game would not be concluded tonight.

When I returned to the hotel I saw some of my colleagues and their wives in the reception area for the meeting I had been at earlier. They said, "We saw you on TV with your sign outside the ballpark before the game!"

I still had my sign and the souvenir baseball cap that was handed out at the gate. More importantly I had the memories of one of the most anticipated nights in sports. Baseball, tradition, and memories — they all go together!

Comisky Park Farewell — 1990

Turning back the clock

It began in 1900 when the White Sox played their first game in a wooden stadium. By 1910, Charles Comisky had built only the third modern steel-and-concrete stadium in the United States. In 1990, the sun set for the last time on the "Baseball Palace of the World." Thus read the 1990 White Sox program. The next year this southside Chicago team would move across the street to the new Comisky Park where the value of nostalgia and "intimacy" of seating could be combined with all the amenities of modern baseball design in the first true hybrid stadium.

As one of the farewells to the eighty-year-old Comisky Park, a

day was set aside to "turn back the clock" to memorialize this old edifice and encourage fans to savor its final season. The date was July 11, 1990, and the day was designed to give the crowd a taste of what it was like there in 1917, the last year the Sox were world champions. The team wore replica uniforms made of modern cloth, but otherwise were dressed like the bygone days.

An insert in the program explained, "No electronic scoreboards today. A manual scoreboard in centerfield has been built just for today, and a megaphone will be used for pre-game line-up. Nanny Forest and her accordion will replace Nanny Forest and her organ. Dixieland musicians, a barbershop quartet, and an organ grinder and monkey are reminiscent of that era's entertainment. General admission tickets are fifty cents, which is about what seats sold for in 1917. Our sponsors have agreed to forego their in-park advertisements in the spirit of the occasion."

The program had a picture of the champion White Sox of 1917. The final statement in the brochure was one I resonated with in 1990, but that foreshadowed trouble in the years ahead. "The faces may have changed many times since 1917, but the game remains the same. Enjoy!" In 1996, two years after the strike and cancellation of the 1994 World Series, baseball is still trying to return to that point where the game "remains the same." I hope it makes it.

On this day my baseball memories were recharged. Flashbacks from forty years ago passed through me, and a stop at the souvenir stand made the experience complete. At $39, a 1917 White Sox cap became my priciest baseball memento up to that point. General admission tickets may have been at 1917 prices, but the merchandisers knew how to price their replicas. That outing may have been a fan's last touch with traditional baseball.

And Then There Was One

Wimbledon — 1996

A Must for the Sports Aficionado

In June 1996, an Air Guard buddy said he would go with me to Wimbledon, the one world-class sporting event I had never attended. Another buddy said he could get tickets through his son-in-law, who was Boris Becker's coach. Neither ever materialized. So I did what came naturally. I went alone. Without a ticket.

Flights were jammed from June 29 through July 10 with the summer crush. I tried routing through Dublin, Manchester, Brussels, and Amsterdam with little hope of success. Flight after flight was booked and had a waiting list.

After much debate on a departure time, I asked Ginger to call at noon on Saturday, June 29, about the flights from Atlanta *that evening* to London. You never know. The 5:25 p.m. flight was oversold by thirty-one, but the 7:55 p.m. flight had six seats remaining in business and seven in coach. The reservation agent was aghast when Ginger said, "My husband is packing now. Would you list him for the 2:15 p.m. flight from Nashville to Atlanta and the 5:25 p.m. flight

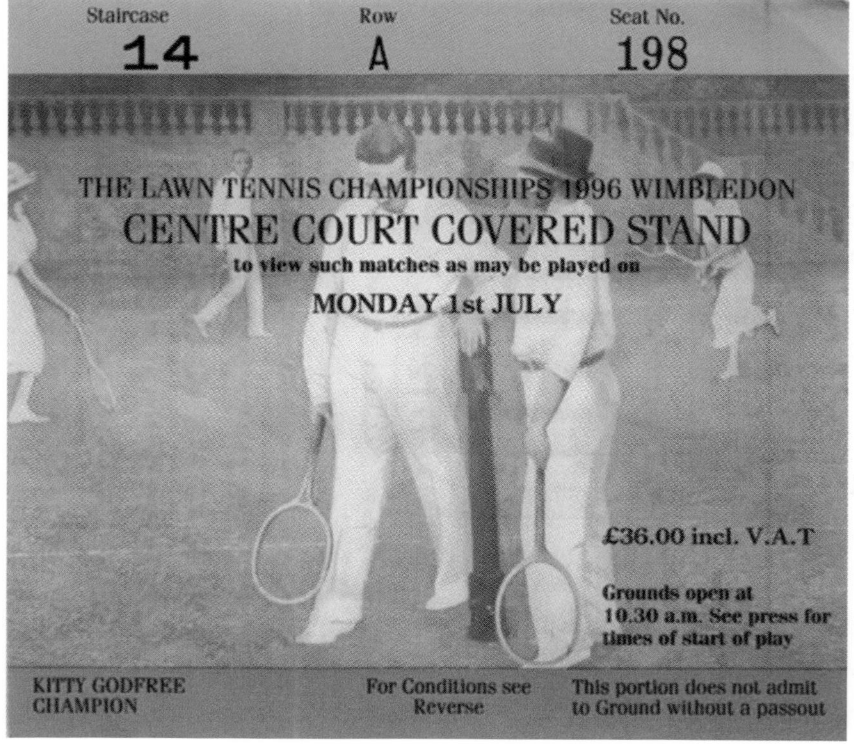

to Gatwick?" It happened that fast. Sunday morning, June 30, at 6:30 a.m., I touched down on Delta Flight 12 at Gatwick. After clearing customs, I headed directly to the local information booth just outside the exit area for arriving international travelers.

When the proper British lady advised me no tennis matches were held on the mid-Sunday of the tournament, I could not believe my oversight — I had arrived a day early. But, as it turned out, that mistake probably saved me from being shut out of a ticket!

After checking in at the Intercontinental at Hyde Park, I went directly to the concierge as a possible ticket source. "Oh, a Center Court ticket for Monday's matches will probably cost £800." Wow!

"What other choices do I have?" I queried. Derek, the concierge, suggested, "You could go out early in the morning and get in the queue. Four hundred tickets will be put on sale for Center Court and Court #1." "How early?" I asked. "Oh, about 5 a.m." I thanked him and went to my room to gather my thoughts and come up with a strategy. This could be devastating, certainly cost prohibitive. Had I come three thousand miles a day early to a sold-out event to be confronted with such options?

As it turned out, arriving a day early was a blessing. That Sunday afternoon I traveled to Southfield, the subway/train station for Wimbledon, a fifteen-minute walk from the station, and found the queues already forming on the sidewalks for Monday's matches. Overnight campers had set up their tents, sleeping bags, shelters, outdoor grills, and portable TVs for the wait until 10:30 a.m. when the ticket windows would open. Families were playing board games, cards, reading, or just visiting. The young groups of men and women were in a festive mode. Nobody seemed bored even in the face of an eighteen-hour wait. Only then would they know if they were lucky enough for Center Court, Court #1, or general admission to the grounds.

I chatted with several in the lines, and asked if they were in line to buy a ticket for resale or for their own use. One lady looked at me as if I were nuts, as if to say, "I am here to watch the best of tennis." Some kept this vigil on an annual basis — a planned family outing. Others seemed to view it as an extended tailgate party similar to what we Americans do for several hours before a big football game.

Signs were prominently displayed saying "Do Not Buy Tickets From Scouts — Strictly Forbidden." There were evidently three ways to gain admission legally: buy from a debenture holder, the ballot, or the queue. The debenture holders could resell their seats without any problem. Patrons who got their tickets by ballot were on a list maintained at the entrance. The holders of those tickets may be asked for identification to verify they are the legitimate owners of those tickets. No ID, no admission. With these limited prospects I pondered my approach.

Back at the hotel I conferred again with Derek. He called his ticket source. A Center Court ticket was available for £1700, approximately $2,500 US. Out of the question. I asked about a ticket to the Grounds — good for sixteen courts and all the amenities offered by the All England Tennis Association Club. He asks his source. "£125 for Grounds and Marquee admission." "I'll take it. I'm not going to this effort and expense to be left without a ticket." Also, I did not want to line up in a queue overnight or have an illegal ticket. All was legal and set for Monday's matches. I asked that the ticket be delivered to the hotel by 8 p.m. If that failed, I'd get up at 3 a.m. to be in the queue by 4.

Since Steffi Graff, Pete Sampras, and the home country favorite Tim Henman would be in the Center Court, the demand for Monday's matches were up. The concierge said that for the Opening Day when a London favorite, Andre Agassi, was playing, the queues formed on Friday evening — three nights in advance of his round!

With ticket in hand, even at such an expensive price, the pressure was off. There would be no complications at the gate on Monday, so I could play tourist on Monday morning. I took a walk across St. James Park to Buckingham Palace, down the Mall to Whitehall past Downing Street to the Cabinet War Room, and a one-hour tour through Churchill's underground command center awaited me. The stroll continued to Westminster Abbey, Big Ben, and Parliament. There I boarded the subway for an early arrival at the Southfield Station to join the crowd for the leisurely walk to the tennis Mecca of the world.

Fortunately for me, I continued past the lines queued for admission. Those for Center Court had long since been admitted, two hundred from each of the two queues on each side of the grounds. Those of us with ducats had short lines in one of the eight or nine entrances. A threat of rain was in the wind, but the patrons, mostly dressed in very presentable attire, ambled outside the courts in a relaxed and happy manner. The semi-permanent food outlets offered an array of pizza, long dark hot dog equivalents, ice cream, beer, Cokes, and Wimbledon's famous strawberries and cream.

Courts 13 and 14 — on either side of Center Court — and Court 1 and Court 2 were hosting the top matches of the day after the premier Center Court. Those three all had reserved seats, and very short queues were forming for Courts 13 and 14 for the unreserved seating to view seeded players and competitive matches. My exploration took me into the new Court 1, under construction and available for the 1997 tournament. A huge concrete venue was nearing completion, the grass already rolled into place and growing.

On the front side of the grounds was a green hillside with picnic tables, benches, and chairs abutting a finished pavilion, along with a walkway on the backside of the New Court 1. A huge TV screen was situated there for all the hillside eaters/drinkers to relax and enjoy their treats and watch one of the on-going matches — Goran Ivanisevic of Croatia and Patrick Rafter of Australia.

On my way to check out the Ticket Resale booth I stopped at Court 14 to watch the number thirteen seed Mary Pierce of France and Elena Likhovtseva of Russia compete in a close match. Their play was interrupted twice by rain delays. During the second shower I left to get in the Ticket Resale queue. The Honorable Steward offered some very excellent advice. "The queue is short now, but come back in an hour or hour-and-half. The line will be longer, but it will move quickly after the first match is completed. Go watch some good tennis at the other courts." What he did not say, but may have worked to my advantage, was that the rain delays influenced some to leave for pre-arranged rides as the afternoon turned to rush hour.

During one of the rain delays I availed myself of the Wimbledon Lawn Tennis Museum, a most interesting walk back through tennis history. Photos, equipment, court evolvement, and video clips of the more recent years accented the saga of tennis and the trail of this tournament, beginning in 1877. It ranks in there with The Open, National League Baseball, America's Cup, and the Triple Crown in terms of longevity. Such tradition is one of the characteristics that attracts me to these events. Wimbledon has enjoyed its success, not forgetting that the sport is the focal point, the athletes on center stage, and the fans deserve to be treated like the customers they are.

While I had paid an exorbitant amount to the event, the face value of a ticket to Center Court was £36 or approximately $55 or $60 US. That was to see three matches between the world's best, both male and female. Not a bad deal. The stewards, gatekeeper, bobbies, merchants, and uniformed military were all there to assist, make me feel welcome, and respond hospitably to my needs and inquires. Even after 119 years, the much maligned British snobbery is subdued. In fact, I thought it was a very fan-friendly group. All of this caused me to ponder the effort and the luck that had preceded in the past forty-eight hours and continued to unfold in this temple of tennis. That made it all worthwhile!

On to Center Court to see the conclusion of the match between Tim Henman, the first Brit to advance this far since 1973, and Magnus Gustafsson of the Netherlands. For £5 at the Resale window I was on Row A on the end of the Court opposite the Royal Box! (Three days ago I hadn't even planned to be here at all!) I guess British Royalty prefers the sun to the shade. As it is so rare, those seats are the primo. I was just thankful to be situated behind the TV cameras in the first four or five rows below my section.

As with any first time attendance at a major championship, you just sit and enjoy the stadium, the crowd, the noise (or in the case of tennis and golf, the peacefulness during the shotmaking) and the wonderment of thanking the Ticket Fairy for making it all possible. How can one guy be so lucky?

The Brit won that afternoon, to the delight of the home crowd, and advanced to the semifinals. His opponent was most gracious in defeat. As an example in the final set, when it was something like 5-4 in games, Gustafsson applauded one of Henman's points after a long, competitive exchange of volleys. Civil, gentlemanly conduct between competitors adds so much to a sport. It reminds me that players understand the game is first. Their best efforts may not be enough, yet they are man enough to recognize and acknowledge when their best shot was superseded by one even better. Somewhere in there is a message, perhaps a principle or moral lesson that we could all pattern. I think it has something to do with the making of a hero. The winners and the heroes are not always ultimately the same.

The only disappointment of the whole excursion was the announcement at 7:30 p.m. "Due to the late hour, it would be unfair to the competitors to commence their match, when there was no chance of completing it before darkness." Top seed Pete Sampras and C. Pioline would start the matches the next day on Center Court. By the time of their first serve, I would be on a Delta MD-11 passing Lands End for an eight-hour forty-five-minute flight to Atlanta.

In this four-day whirlwind trip to Wimbledon I reached the pinnacle of tennis championships. In 1994, I had raced to the U.S. Tennis Open thinking that was the best, and, in the U.S., it is. But since that trip I've had this gnawing in my subconscious: Wimbledon was the major prize in tennis, if not by longevity and standing, certainly by the fan appeal of the NBC telecasts of this Fourth of July tradition.

I was relieved! The delay of my book until after the '96 Olympics was a blessing in disguise. There was no chink in the armor, in my view, as to now having attended the premier championships in at least eleven sports — football (2), baseball, basketball (2), hockey, golf (4), tennis, auto racing (2), horse racing (3), soccer, boxing, and sailing, plus the Winter and Summer Olympics — twenty-one sporting championships. These are a portion of my Top 25 sporting events.

My favorites follow.

Personal Favorites

After identifying my criteria for a major sporting championship, I have often been asked to identify my most favorite sporting contests.

The following characteristics influence me in arriving at my favorite sporting events:

- ■ Competition is the focal point.
- ■ Consideration for the fans:
  - ● Good viewing.
  - ● Size of arena, without sacrificing proximity to team.
  - ● No or minimal price gouging.
  - ● Volunteer workers with:
    - • love of sport;
    - • dedication to their community or particular event.
  - ● Minimal corporate visibility.
  - ● Venue friendly.
  - ● Opportunity for good seats on game day.
  - ● Opportunity to mingle with athletes.

■ Finally, would I go every year, if I had a ticket? That is the question I answer. I would attend the following ten events every year, with the substitutes marked by asterisks.

Event	*Sport*
Masters	Golf
Final Four	Basketball
Rose Bowl*	Football
Kentucky Derby	Horse racing
Wimbledon	Tennis
Stanley Cup	Hockey
Brickyard 400	Auto racing
America's Cup	Sailing
College World Series**	Baseball
Olympics	One of a kind

* If the Redskins were in the Super Bowl, I would prefer it over the Rose Bowl.

** If the Detroit Tigers were in the World Series, I would prefer it over College World Series.

Boxing and soccer are not included in my favorites; these are replaced with America's Cup.

The Making of a Major

After fifty years of watching the major sporting events in the world and the not-so-major games, I developed my Top 25 Major Sporting Events. A debate will follow among some sports purists and will probably offend aficionados of a few very popular sports, especially emerging events. Some events go unquestioned in terms of their popularity, esteem, and competitiveness.

Over the years the criteria for inclusion in my Top 25 have evolved to these factors:

- Championship in a major sport.
- Fan interest.
- Tradition.
- Changing times. Is the event rising or falling in prestige?
- Duration.
- Number of participants competing for the Cup.

My sports interests began with college football and basketball, professional baseball, and golf, hence my original favorites. Our world expands and our interests follow, thus the inclusion of professional football, basketball, hockey, horse racing, tennis, auto racing, soccer, and the Olympics, the Winter and Summer games. These twenty-five major events have now generated fifty-six personal experiences in gaining a ticket to some life-long memories. Early on I decided if there was something that I wanted to watch, I did not wait for an invitation or wait until next year or wait for a more convenient time.

To the reader, I encourage you to do the same. Overcome the passive tendency to delay or postpone to a later date. If the urge is there, do it! I did not want to wait to reach old age, or that phase of life when either the will or the energy to witness these events had passed. The rocking chairs and nursing homes are replete with persons who lament, wishing they had done so and so when they were able to go. Part of my passion is to avoid at least a portion of that potential regret.

Don't wait — go see these events today! And it's more fun to share the adventure with a child or grandchild. Be a hero to one of them!

This Sports Aficionado's Top 25 Sporting Events

- All-Star baseball game
- America's Cup
- Brickyard 400
- Fiesta Bowl
- Final Four
- Golf's Grand Slam
  - Masters
  - U.S. Open
  - British Open
  - PGA
- Indy 500
- NBA Finals
- Orange Bowl
- Rose Bowl
- Stanley Cup
- Sugar Bowl
- Summer Olympics
- Super Bowl
- Triple Crown
  - Kentucky Derby
  - Preakness
  - Belmont Stakes
- Wimbledon
- Winter Olympics
- World Cup
- World Heavyweight Championship
- World Series

Index of Tickets